AFRICAN
HORIZONS

Recent Titles in
Contributions in Afro-American and African Studies

The Gong and the Flute: African Literary Development and Celebration
Kalu Ogbaa, editor

Masters of the Drum: Black Lit/oratures Across the Continuum
Robert Elliot Fox

Africa's Agenda: The Legacy of Liberalism and Colonialism in the Crisis of
African Values
Harvey J. Sindima

Negritude and Literary Criticism: The History and Theory of "Negro-African" Literature
in French
Belinda Elizabeth Jack

Prospects for Recovery and Sustainable Development in Africa
Aguibou Y. Yansané, editor

The Black Press in the Middle West, 1865–1985
Henry Lewis Suggs, editor

Of Dreams Deferred, Dead or Alive: African Perspectives on African-American Writers
Femi Ojo-Ade

Digging the Africanist Presence in American Performance: Dance and Other Contexts
Brenda Dixon Gottschild

Development Strategies in Africa: Current Economic, Socio-Political, and Institutional
Trends and Issues
Aguibou Y. Yansané, editor

Langston Hughes: Folk Dramatist in the Protest Tradition, 1921–1943
Joseph McLaren

The Rules of the Game: Struggles in Black Recreation and Social Welfare Policy in
South Africa
Alan Gregor Cobley

The Problem of Embodiment in Early African American Narrative
Katherine Fishburn

AFRICAN HORIZONS

The Landscapes of African Fiction

Christine Loflin

Contributions in Afro-American and African Studies, Number 184

Greenwood Press
Westport, Connecticut • London

Library of Congress Cataloging-in-Publication Data

Loflin, Christine, 1959–
    African horizons : the landscapes of African fiction / Christine
Loflin.
        p.   cm. — (Contributions in Afro-American and African
studies, ISSN 0069–9624 ; no. 184)
    Includes bibliographical references (p.   ) and index.
    ISBN 0–313–29733–9 (alk. paper)
    1. African fiction (English)—History and criticism.   2. Landscape
in literature.   3. Land use in literature.   4. Africa—In
literature.   5. Landscape—Africa.   6. Land use—Africa.   I. Title.
II. Series.
    PR9344.L64   1998
    823.009′32—dc21   97–9382

British Library Cataloguing in Publication Data is available.

Library of Congress Catalog Card Number: 97–9382
ISBN: 0–313–29733–9
ISSN: 0069–9624

First published in 1998

Greenwood Press, 88 Post Road West, Westport, CT 06881
An imprint of Greenwood Publishing Group, Inc.

Printed in the United States of America

The paper used in this book complies with the
Permanent Paper Standard issued by the National
Information Standards Organization (Z39.48–1984).

10 9 8 7 6 5 4 3 2 1

Copyright Acknowledgments

The author and publisher gratefully acknowledge permission to reprint the following previously published material:

Excerpts from Lemuel Johnson, Obioma Nnaemeka, Zaynab Alkali, Mariama Bâ, and Miriam Tlali used with permission of the authors, their agents, or publishers.

Excerpts from *Waiting for the Barbarians* by J. M. Coetzee. Copyright © 1980 by J. M. Coetzee. Used by permission of Viking Penguin, a division of Penguin Books USA Inc., and Reed Consumer Books Ltd. Originally published in London: Martin Secker & Warburg, 1980.

Excerpts from *July's People* by Nadine Gordimer. Copyright © 1981 by Nadine Gordimer. Used by permission of Viking Penguin, a division of Penguin Books USA Inc., and A. P. Watt Ltd. on behalf of Nadine Gordimer.

Excerpts from *A Gesture of Belonging: Letters from Bessie Head, 1965–1979*, edited by Randolph Vigne. Copyright © The Estate of Bessie Head, 1996.

Excerpts from Ngugi wa Thiong'o, *The River Between*. London: Heinemann, 1965, reprinted by permission of Heinemann Publishers (Oxford) Limited.

Excerpts from *Petals of Blood* by Ngugi wa Thiong'o. Copyright © 1977 by Ngugi wa Thiong'o. Used by permission of Dutton Signet, a division of Penguin Books USA Inc., and Heinemann Educational, a division of Reed Educational and Professional Publishing Ltd.

Excerpts from *Aké: The Years of Childhood* by Wole Soyinka. Copyright © 1982 by Random House, Inc. Reprinted by permission of Random House, Inc.

Every reasonable effort has been made to trace the owners of copyright materials in this book, but in some instances this has proven impossible. The author and publisher will be glad to receive information leading to more complete acknowledgments in subsequent printings of the book and in the meantime extend their apologies for any omissions.

Contents

Preface   ix

Introduction   1

Chapter 1   Ngugi wa Thiong'o's Visions of Africa   17

Chapter 2   Mother Africa: African Women and the Land   35
             in West African Literature

Chapter 3   The Landscape of Religion in West African   55
             Literature by Men

Chapter 4   "In the Land of a Dying Illusion": The Landscape   71
             of Black South African Township Novels

Chapter 5   Women Writers at Home and in Exile: The Examples   85
             of Bessie Head and Miriam Tlali

Chapter 6   "And Then the Bush Avenged Itself ": The Landscape   101
             of White South African Fiction

Select Bibliography   115

Index   121

Preface

This project is the result of several years' research in Wisconsin, Nigeria, England, South Africa, and Iowa. I am particularly grateful to the librarians at the University of Wisconsin-Madison, the British Museum, the University of Ibadan, the University of Illinois at Champaign-Urbana, and Grinnell College for their help in locating rare and out-of-print materials.

I am very grateful to Bryn Mawr College for its Commonwealth Africa Fellowship, which allowed me to do research at the University of Ibadan, the University of Nigeria, and the University of Nairobi in 1990-91; to my colleagues at the University of Wisconsin-Madison, the University of Ibadan, and Grinnell College; to the members of the NEH Summer Institute on African Literature at the University of Illinois in Champaign-Urbana; and to Grinnell College and the University of Wisconsin-Madison African Studies Program for support to finish my research on this manuscript.

Chapter 1, "Ngugi wa Thiong'o's Visions of Africa" was first presented at the Modern Languages Association of Nigeria's 8th annual conference at the University of Nigeria, February, 1991; a revised version has been published in *Research in African Literature* (Fall 1995). I am grateful to *RAL* for permission to republish it here. Chapter 2, "Mother Africa: African Women and the Land in West African Literature" was originally read at the First International Conference on Women in Africa and the African Diaspora, at the University of Nigeria, July 1992. A portion of Chapter 5, under the title, "The Landscape of Exile: Bessie Head's *Maru* and *A Question of Power*" was read at the African Literature Association conference, Brock University, Ontario, Canada, May 1992. The comments and suggestions of my audiences have led to significant changes in the completed manuscript.

Finally, I wish to thank Charlotte Bruner, Tequia Burt, Jay Clayton, Trisha Howell, Erin Hustings, and Jim Kissane for their careful readings of and comments on my manuscript; to Dennis Brutus, Margaret Daymond, Lemuel Johnson, Margaret Lenta, and Obioma Nnaemeka for conversations which led my work in new directions; to Terri Phipps for her help in the preparation of this manuscript, and to Jim and Jeffrey Dillon, for their patience and companionship.

Introduction

The description of landscape is an overlooked yet highly contested site of cultural expression in African literature in English. Landscape descriptions provide the geographic, cultural, political and social boundaries of the text; the spaces within which the text will signify.[1] Yet, curiously, there has not been an examination of the importance of landscape in African literature. In fact, it was a commonplace of Western criticism of early African literature in English that Africans didn't write about landscape:

Local description was rare, couched in the diction of an alien tradition, and unevocative of an authentic sense of place and time. (Roscoe, *Mother Is Gold* 36)

Indeed, it is extremely difficult to find a passage of pure description of a natural setting anywhere in Anglophone African writing of the first generation. (Larson, *The Emergence of African Fiction* 44)

In both these passages, the authors asserted that landscape was rare in African literature in English. Unintentionally, however, these passages also reveal *why* landscape was so hard for these critics to find in African literature. "Landscape description" evidently meant a detailed passage lauding the beauties of a natural landscape, a literary parallel to European and American landscape paintings in which human figures were peripheral or even absent. Roscoe suggested that, when attempted, landscape descriptions were obvious imitations of Western description, "inauthentic." Larson's comment, on the other hand, implied that landscape descriptions did not resemble their predecessors enough; African writers did not write passages of "pure description." By using European and American literature as a standard for judging African literature, both Roscoe and Larson created a theoretical dilemma for African writing in English: the closer African writing was to the ideal Western mode of description, the more it became "inauthentic." In short, Western critics such as Roscoe and Larson used a contradictory set of prescriptions which by their very nature denied the possibility of "authentic" landscape description in African literature.

Western critics were expecting to find the African novel an immature version of European literature, showing promise in those areas where it most closely imitated the European tradition. Yet this standard made it almost impossible for African writers to fulfill critics' demands for detailed description of space in the novel, as Chinweizu argues in *Toward the Decolonization of African Literature*. Western critics wanted novels to be "universal" in their themes. C. B. Robson claimed that Ngugi wa Thiong'o's *The River Between* was about the universal struggle of mankind against oppression (Robson 129); Charles Larson praised Lenrie Peters' *The Second Round* for its universality: "If a few names of characters and places were changed one would indeed feel that this was an American novel or a French or Italian novel. In short, Peters' story is universal" (Larson 230). For these critics, precise description of landscape became "local color," as Chinweizu argues:

This matter of precise spatial location has been regularly misused by "universalist" critics, especially when they accuse African novels of "local color." They choose to forget that in describing an African setting, you can't meet their call for precise spatio-temporal location at the same time as their absurd demand for a "universal" setting (meaning, outside Africa). . . . Clearly, the game of literary criticism is being played, at least on African literature, in bad faith. (Chinweizu 105)

If African writers described the landscape in detail, they were indulging in "local color";[2] if they did not, then they were failing to write a great novel according to the standards of the Western novel tradition. "Authentic" landscape description, by definition, could not be found in African fiction.

Western critics also were expecting to find descriptions of Africa that continued the tradition of European representations of Africa as the Dark Continent. Writers such as William Burchell in his *Travels in the Interior of Southern Africa*, David Livingstone in *Missionary Travels and Researches in Southern Africa*, and Mary Kingsley in her *Travels in West Africa* describe the African landscape in detail, reveling in its differences from the civilized European landscape. They emphasize the isolation of their European sensibilities within an almost inhuman landscape, beautiful, exotic, unmistakably Other. Other twentieth century Western writers, from Joseph Conrad to Isak Dinesen, create an African landscape as an ideal backdrop for their explorations of the deficiencies of contemporary Western culture; the African landscape becomes a huge, exotic canvas for their essentially European narratives. In these texts, the presence of Africans within the landscape is minimized or even ignored. Because of this tradition, Western critics of African literature expected the African landscape to be described as exotic, even by writers for whom this was familiar home ground. They also expected these descriptions to follow not only the themes, but also the pattern of travel description. As in Burchell, Kingsley or Conrad, in African literature by Africans the reader should be presented with a single observer describing a wide sweep of landscape, uninhabited, isolated and romantic: "There it is before you— smiling, frowning, inviting, grand, mean, insipid, or savage, and always mute with an air of whispering, Come and find out" (Conrad, *Heart of Darkness* 27). The landscape of Africa, as Christopher Miller has observed, is seen as a blank slate, which can represent whatever the Western observer wishes to inscribe on it.

When African writers began writing in European languages, these descriptions of Africa from a Western perspective were already well-established; in their works, African writers sought to assert the validity of their own visions of the African landscape. Yet even some African writers agreed with the idea that there was only a limited place for landscape description in African fiction. Despite Chinweizu's spirited defense of African literature, he tacitly concedes the lack of landscape description in his claim that "if African readers don't feel that the descriptions, portraits and characterizations supplied by their writers are sketchier than they would like, the objections of Westerners, with their alien sensibilities, won't matter" (Chinweizu 123). Miriam Tlali, commenting about her own writing, remarks: "I don't think I should at this time in our history be involved in a lot of talking and dreaming about the beautiful skies and the moon" (Tlali, interview in *Between the Lines* 76). These comments reinforce the assumption that landscape description is about isolated, romantic visions of the natural landscape, "the beautiful skies and the moon."

The position I take in this study, however, is that African writers do describe the African landscape. Characters in African fiction are always carefully situated within their environment. The description of that environment is extremely varied and differs from the European model, especially in its insistence on the inclusion of the human community within the natural world. For example, in J. P. Clark's poem, "Ibadan," the focus is on an urban landscape:

> Ibadan,
>   running splash of rust
> and gold —flung and scattered
> among seven hills like broken
> china in the sun. (Clark 57)

The specific geographic identity of the Ibadan landscape, the seven hills, are indicated, but the emphasis is on the human community, the flashing of light off the rusted metal roofs of Ibadan's buildings. Clark also suggests Ibadan's history as a place of refuge for its first settlers, and its uncontrolled expansion, in the image of the broken china "flung and scattered among seven hills." Clark sets Ibadan, not only within its African geographic and temporal situation, but also within its postcolonial historical space; the seven hills, while a reference to Ibadan's location, simultaneously evoke the seven hills of Rome, the symbolic center of Western civilization and colonization. Thus the "seven hills" are an overdetermined signifier, pointing both to *this* place, Ibadan, and to Rome.

Ibadan's colonization is further reflected in the poem's references to "rust" and "broken china,"—metal roofing and china were products introduced by the British in Nigeria; their presence reminds the reader of this history, while their rusted and broken condition is a remarkably terse comment on the aftereffects of colonialism. Despite this grim history, the poem reflects the speaker's love for this landscape, in the emphasis upon the flashing light of the sun, reflected by the rooftops of Ibadan.

Ibadan's overwritten, overdetermined landscape was part of my own experience of the city and the University of Ibadan when I was there in 1990-1991. The campus contains examples of both Western architectural styles and African designs which incorporate sculpture, mosaics and African symbolic ornaments; the most dramatic example of the latter is the Institute of African Studies. Even the names of the students' halls, from Queen Elizabeth Hall to Tafewa Balewa Hall, reveal the colonial and postcolonial history of the nation. Religion, also, has played a role: the Anglican Cathedral on campus has erected a huge cross, dominating an intersection. It stands directly east of the campus mosque (and thus in the direction Muslims face when they pray within the mosque). To counter this monument, the Muslim community has built a freestanding wall between the cross and the mosque, a visible representation of their resistance to the Christian religious symbol. Yet the campus is also marked by an absence: while there are several churches and the mosque on campus, there are no buildings or sites officially dedicated to the practice of Yoruba or other traditional Nigerian religions, as Wole Soyinka noted in a Spring 1991 talk on the University campus. The landscape is not, cannot be, an apolitical space. From the imposing Faculty Club with its cracked and empty swimming pool to the roadside ditches where in 1991 University workers were preparing to lay pipe lines, as a result of student riots over the water supply the summer before, the landscape revealed the influence of human conflict and compromise. The trees themselves were a combination of native and exotic species; the crops planted by the agricultural students were both native West African and introduced species from the Americas; and the grass, while native, was cut to resemble European lawns, by gardeners who labored with machetes. Reading this landscape, and remembering the integral role that specific features of the landscape play in many traditional African religions, I realized that landscape in African fiction reflects this complex, overdetermined, often even conflicting matrix of colonial, precolonial and postcolonial history, and contemporary political, economic, and social relationships. The European image of a landscape distinct from the human community must be abandoned, so that the significance of landscape in African fiction can emerge.

In this study, I use the term "landscape" to explore, not only pristine, so-called natural landscapes, landscapes which I will argue are also always embedded within a social discourse, but also the landscapes which are obviously affected by the human communities which build and sustain them: the landscapes of rural life, of villages, and of cities. I will also argue that we should consider the significance of interior domestic landscapes, especially in the works of women writers, who reveal the importance of this space for their female characters. My project will explore the ways that African writers reveal through their fictional land-scapes the social, political, economic, and religious history of Africa.

Beyond the immediate, visible horizon of landscape, African writers also situate their characters within the larger horizons of nation, ethnicity, race, and international political and economic relations. These horizons establish the limits within which the novel will signify. For some writers, such as Ngugi wa Thiong'o, the nation-space will be the most significant horizon of the novel; for others, the local community or the horizon of the African continent itself will be more important boundaries than that of the nation. Some African writers limit the geography of their texts to the boundaries of the European metropole and the colonized African state; others place themselves within the transnational community of the African diaspora. Through their depictions of these larger horizons of their fiction, African writers situate their texts within complex geographies of international connections and geopolitical power.

African writers' descriptions of the African landscape are interventions in a historical dialogue about the meaning and significance of Africa, African peoples, and African land. Thus the continuing debates over the interpretation of Africa's precolonial, colonial and postcolonial history are part of the context of the interpretation of these literary texts. I provide here a short description of current debates about the interpretation of the history of Africa as a background for my interpretation of landscape in African fiction.

PRECOLONIAL AFRICA

Precolonial Africa was initially considered by Westerners to be the epitome of primitive, savage cultures, "darkest Africa." In response to this image, early African writers insisted on the importance of the civilizations of precolonial Africa and their significant cultural, political, and religious achievements. Later writers, in support of their attempts to define a foundation for Pan-African unity, identified certain social traits and philosophical ideas as integral to all African cultures. Precolonial African history is often invoked to support or challenge contemporary political and cultural theories.

A significant factor in precolonial African history was the relative ease of migration: "In many parts of Africa, people have traditionally manifested their discontent with the existing political community by migrating where they can live unhindered by their former rulers" (Herbst 183). Open land and traditional agricultural practices which required migration encouraged people to exercise this option; regimes which were unpopular gradually lost population through migration. This pattern changed dramatically with the advent of colonialism and the imposition of national boundaries on the map of Africa.

In literature, writers such as Chinua Achebe and Ngugi wa Thiong'o have looked to oral traditions of precolonial history to locate their characters not only within a Westernized, colonized African space, but also within the imagined community of a specific cultural tradition. In their fiction, Achebe, Ngugi and others establish the traditional communal and religious significance of the local landscape, using it as one of many interpretive systems within their work. South African writers have a more complicated relationship with traditional culture because of the specific strategies of the South African government under apartheid. Between 1948 and 1990, the South African government deliberately tried to emphasize cultural and ethnic identity over racial identity, creating the "homelands" within the borders of South Africa and encouraging the separation of different ethnicities. Protesting against this policy, many black South African writers have emphasized their race rather than their ethnicity as the most distinctive factor in their identity, and emphasize the nation rather than the village or the ethnic community as the most significant boundary in their fiction. Precolonial South African history, however, is alluded to in both black and white fiction from South Africa; often, it is interpreted as an African past which, by its very presence, implies a nonwhite, African future.

COLONIALISM AND IMPERIALISM

According to Edward Said, "modern European imperialism itself is a constitutively and a radically different type of overseas domination from all earlier forms" ("Yeats and Decolonization" 71). Not only the scale, but the longevity of the disparity of power between First and Third World nations, its organization, and its penetration into the details of everyday life set it apart from previous empires. European colonialism systematically underdeveloped Africa: "Colonialism was not merely a system of exploitation, but one whose essential purpose was to repatriate the profits to the so-called 'mother country'" (Rodney 162). European colonialism also had an enormous cultural impact, subordinating the Other to the culture of Europe: "This cultural process has to be seen if not as the origin and cause, then at least as the vital, informing, and invigorating counterpoint to the economic and political machinery that we all concur stands at the center of imperialism" (Said 72). The relationship of imperialism to landscape then is twofold. Most of Africa was held in some kind of economic and political subjugation to Europe. Europeans were the owners of Africa (Belgian King Leopold II's personal ownership of the Congo is the most egregious example). Through this ownership, and the resultant exploitation of African resources, the landscape of Africa was irrevocably changed. State boundaries, roads, bridges, mines, and plantations were all imposed on the African land: "Imperialism after all is an act of geographical violence through which virtually every space in the world is explored, charted, and finally brought under control" (Said 77). In addition to this, narratives of explorers, missionaries, and colonial officers all superimpose on Africa their own Eurocentric visions of development, progress, and civilization. According to Benedict Anderson,

the late colonial state's style of thinking about its domain . . . was a totalizing classificatory grid, which could be applied with endless flexibility to anything under the state's real or contemplated control: peoples, regions, religions, languages, products, monuments and so forth. (Anderson 184)

This kind of "thinking" is reflected in the desire of Conrad's Marlow to visit one of the "blank spots" of the earth. It denies to the colony its particularity of topography, history, and religion; every aspect of the colonial environment is assumed to be classifiable, and hence it is subsumed under a European system. In response to this, "there is a pressing need for the recovery of the land that, because of the presence of the colonizing outsider, is recoverable at first only through the imagination" (Said 77). Pre-independence novels such as Chinua Achebe's *Things Fall Apart* represent the imaginative recapturing of the colonized African space.

NATIONALISM

Recently, there has been a resurgence of interest in nationalism in contemporary theory which challenges earlier definitions of the nation-state. In these texts, the nation-state is recognized as a comparatively recent phenomenon: "It was only as late as the nineteenth century that the idea became widely accepted that the proper boundaries of the state should coincide, not with the particular territory that had been historically acquired by dynastic alliance or conquest, but with a given people, who constituted a *nation*." (Beetham 208-209). While nations may claim ancient roots, their real claim to legitimacy is based on modern political concepts. E. J. Hobsbawm claims that nations must be historically located, because the existence of the nation is predicated on the existence of particular technologies and economic developments, particularly printing, mass literacy, and mass schooling (Hobsbawm 3). Thus nations are not just geographical, but also temporal spaces. Homi K. Bhabha defines the nation in the following way:

The political unity of the nation consists in a continual displacement of its irredeemably plural modern space, bounded by different, even hostile nations, into a signifying space that is archaic and mythical, paradoxically representing the nation's modern territoriality, in the patriotic, atavistic temporality of Traditionalism. (Bhabha 300)

By Bhabha's definition, the nation is not just the monolithic narrative of nationalism, building patriotism through the invocation of a myth of origin, but is also "irredeemably plural." The narrative of nation, by its very nature as a reconfiguration of history and identity, in itself implies that other narratives are possible. Bhabha claims: "The nation reveals, in its ambivalent and vacillating representation, the ethnography of its own historicity and opens up the possibility of other narratives of the people and their difference" (Bhabha 300).[3] This process has been acted out on the international scene with the fragmentation of the republics of the former Soviet Union.

Where Bhabha seeks contradictions and inconsistencies within nationalism that will lead to its own collapse (the places within the narrative of nationalism that point to the existence of an irreducibly plural, heterogeneous society), Said looks to something beyond nationalism, which he tentatively calls "liberation," to move beyond nationalism's nativistic and repressive tendencies:

It is in this phase that I would like to suggest that *liberation,* and not nationalist independence, is the new alternative, liberation which by its very nature involves, in Fanon's words, a transformation of social consciousness beyond national consciousness. ("Yeats and Decolonization" 83)[4]

According to Benedict Anderson, nationalism in the European colonies arose in a different set of historical circumstances than European nationalism: "The 'last wave' of nationalisms, most of them in the colonial territories of Asia and Africa, was in its origins a response to the new-style global imperialism made possible by the achievements of industrial capitalism" (Anderson 139). The colonial elite had access to the models of nation and nationalism from America and Europe, which they copied and adapted to suit their own purposes: "the nation was becoming an international norm, and . . . it was possible to 'model' nationness in a much more complex way than hitherto" (Anderson 139). In some colonial territories, states existed before nations did: "Many of these new states were highly artificial constructions, states in search of nations still to be formed, in which the only national force remaining after the decay of the nationalist movements has been the army and the state bureaucracy" (Beetham 209).

A further complication of the "last wave" of nationalism is its interdependence with the narratives of colonialism and imperialism which preceded it:

At some stage in the antiresistance phase of nationalism there is a sort of dependence between the two sides of the contest, since after all many of the nationalist struggles were led by bourgeoisies that were partly formed and to some degree produced by the colonial power; these are the national bourgeoisies of which Fanon spoke so ominously. (Said 74)

In many African countries, these elites became the new leaders of independent Africa, only to continue many of the policies of the colonial powers. Nationalism became neocolonialism, and failed to change the living circumstances of the majority of African people.

Because the boundaries of African nations were drawn by the European imperial powers, there is something inherently artificial about the landscape of nationalism in Africa. Boundaries divide ethnic and linguistic groups, and unite historically antagonistic peoples. Despite this history, however, the nation-state in Africa cannot be simply wished away: "The colonial state cannot be captured and appropriated except as a nation state. It only remains to be asked what *kind* of nation state" (Lazarus 76). Neil Lazarus concludes his argument by insisting that "it is only on the terrain of the nation that an articulation between cosmopolitan intellectualism and popular consciousness can be forged . . . [and] imperialism can be overthrown" (Lazarus 91-92). Lazarus, by pointing to the struggles of the Palestinian and South African peoples, provides a warning against too easily dismissing nationalism as a liberating factor in contemporary history.

Ngugi wa Thiong'o insists on the importance of the national space in Kenya, as I show in Chapter 1. In his work, national identity is meant to supersede ethnic and linguistic divisions, uniting Kenyans in a socialist state. Ngugi never denies the problematic origins of the nation-state of Kenya in the colonial period, but he insists that there can be no return to a precolonial tribal organization. Instead, Kenyans must accept nationalism as a precondition for socialism.

WOMEN AND NATIONALISM

The horizon of the nation-state is only one possible horizon of a literary text. It may be questioned, limited, or even delegitimized as a significant boundary for the text by the presentation of alternative horizons, such as ethnic boundaries, transnational communities, or the boundary of the local community.   For women writers in particular, the space of the nation may be problematic, or inaccessible.[5]

Virginia Woolf, in *Three Guineas*, claims that women are stateless: "As a woman, I have no country. As a woman I want no country. As a woman my country is the whole world" (Woolf 109). Elleke Boehmer, in her essay "Stories of Women and Mothers: Gender and Nationalism in the Early Fiction of Flora Nwapa," shows that women's relationship to the nation is further problematized by the gendered discourse of nationalism: "Figures of mothers of the nation are everywhere emblazoned but the presence of women in the nation is officially marginalised and generally ignored" (Boehmer 6). In Africa, the nation-space is often made inaccessible to women through African nationalism's use of the rhetoric of traditionalism in defending its nationalist goals: African nationalism in this myth involves the restoration of a precolonial African state, in which women's role is to be the "bearer of nationalist sons" (Boehmer 8).   Women who challenge this mythology run the risk of being considered anti-African and unpatriotic.

In Chapter 2, I show that the nation-space is de-emphasized in West African women's writing. Rather, these writers focus on the intimate space of the family, the public space of the village, and international forces which form the horizon of individual and familial experience. Boehmer claims that African women's writing explores the multiplicities of identities offered by these different horizons: "Given that men have monopolized the field of nationalist identity and self-image, women may thus have to evolve other strategies of selving—perhaps less unitary; perhaps more dispersed and multifarious" (Boehmer 9).

Woolf's claim that "as a woman, I have no country" suggests that women, excluded from the public sphere, can exist apart from it. According to Gayatri Spivak, however, women cannot set aside nationalist ideology so easily; it is inevitably a part of their vision of the world, an interpretive grid that places nation at the center: "One cannot of course 'choose' to step out of ideology" (Spivak 120). The critique of nationalist ideology by women will always be a critique from the inside. Rachel Blau DuPlessis suggests that this insider/outsider position creates a female aesthetic: "Her ontological, her psychic, her class position all cause doubleness. Doubled consciousness. Doubled understandings. How then could she neglect to invent a form which produces this incessant, critical, splitting motion" (DuPlessis 278). DuPlessis then links this doubleness to the position of other Others: "What we here have been calling (the) female aesthetic turns out to be a specialized name for . . . all social practices which wish to criticize, to differentiate from, to overturn the dominant forms of knowing and understanding with which they are saturated" (DuPlessis 285). Thus women's position as insider/outsider is similar to the predicament of any postcolonial writer; splitting, fragmentation, and hybridity are the signs of this presence.

While Spivak insists on the impossibility of women being outside ideology, she also maintains that the nation-state cannot be the outer limit of public discourse, especially for women. In "Feminism and Critical Theory" Spivak describes the imprisonment and beatings suffered by South Korean women who went on strike for a better wage at a factory owned by Control Data, a company based in Minnesota. In her analysis, she points out the multiple relations of power inherent in the situation: a First World company making use of the labor pool of the Third World; the South Korean government's encouragement of such companies to improve the economy; and the women's husbands' desire to keep their wives' salaries lower than their own, to "save face" (Spivak 89-91). An analysis of these women's situation which emphasized the horizon of the nation-state would be inadequate, and might even conclude that the suppression of the strike was necessary, in support of the national economy and "traditional" culture. According to Spivak, then, an analysis of the position of women in the Third World must take into account the effects of global capitalism: "for reasons of collusion between pre-existing structures of patriarchy and transnational capitalism, it is the urban sub-proletarian female who is the paradigmatic subject of the current configuration of the International Division of Labor" (Spivak 218).

The works of fiction in this study enter into national and international discourse in different, even contradictory ways. In Chapter 5, I read Miriam Tlali and Bessie Head's work in relation to the nation-states of South Africa and Botswana. Both writers' works situate their characters within the horizons of the contemporary nation, but also redraw the boundaries of the state. The landscapes and horizons of their texts attempt to provide a wider horizon than the boundaries of the nation-state and a vision of a future state in which racial and tribal prejudices will be eliminated.

EXILE AND EXPATRIATION

One effect of colonialism and imperialism has been the disruption and dislocation of individuals, families, even entire populations. A multitude of factors has created the extraordinary motility of colonial and postcolonial states, in addition to the migratory practices of precolonial societies discussed previously. In particular, the forced expulsion of political exiles from South Africa and elsewhere has added to the flow of migrants, expatriates, and immigrants; as Bhabha describes them, "wandering peoples who will not be contained within the *Heim* of the national culture and its unisonant discourse, but are themselves the marks of a shifting boundary" (Bhabha 315). Virtually all of the writers in this study have experienced some form of exile.

Even within one's native country, one can experience exile and alienation. In Africa, the use of English already involves a "translation" of experience, a distancing of the sort Christopher Miller describes in Francophone literature. Further, the privileging of the metropole, of a Home Country that is not home, destabilizes and disrupts one's sense of place. As the Caribbean writer Jamaica Kincaid comments,

We understood then—we were meant to understand then—that England was to be our source of myth and the source from which we got our sense of reality, our sense of what was meaningful, our sense of what was meaningless—and much about our own lives and much about the very idea of us headed that last list. (Kincaid 32)

This dislocation of culture under colonialism is at the heart of the struggle for identity in early African postcolonial texts.

Salman Rushdie describes the predicament of the exiled writer in "Imaginary Homelands":

If we do look back, we must also do so in the knowledge—which gives rise to pro-found uncertainties—that our physical alienation from India almost inevitably means that we will not be capable of reclaiming precisely the thing that was lost; that we will, in short, create fictions, not actual cities or villages, but invisible ones, imagi-nary homelands, Indias of the mind. (Rushdie 10)

The writer is in exile, not only from the contemporary homeland which moves further and further away in time from the remembered homeland, but also from the remembered homeland itself, which becomes a fiction. The rhetorical role of the "imaginary homeland" exceeds the mere recollection of the historical past; it is that fictional Archimedean point from which the exiled writer measures and moves the world.

Alex La Guma and Ngugi wa Thiong'o were exiled by the governments of their home countries; Buchi Emecheta chose expatriation in England. Most of the writers in this study have experienced periods of voluntary or involuntary exile. A few, like Emecheta, become immigrants, while others, such as Ngugi, remain adamantly expatriate. Occasionally, writers celebrate the freedom of ex-ile, the freedom to experiment, to voice what was silenced in the home country. Others experience what Joseph Brodsky calls the tragicomedy of the exiled writer: "The democracy into which he has arrived provides him with physical safety but renders him socially insignificant. And the lack of significance is what no writer, exile or not, can take" (Brodsky, qtd. in Broe 1).

Exile and expatriation may have a different effect on women writers. Shari Benstock, in "Expatriate Modernism," claims "the definitions of *exile* and *expa-triate* were different for men and women, were experienced differently by them" (Benstock 23). Already expatriated by their gender in their home country, Mod-ernist women writers in France "were freed to write out the internalized expatria-tion against which they had always defined themselves" (Benstock 28). Thus exile might provide a double liberation for women, allowing them to express their feelings of alienation already experienced within the home country. For an

African woman writer in exile such as Buchi Emecheta, her distance from her home country may be a necessary distance, allowing her to express the limitations of women's roles which she experienced and observed within Nigeria. On the other hand, Bessie Head's experiences in exile in Botswana challenged her assumptions about black Africa; she had expected to be welcomed, as if back to her home country, when she left South Africa. Head's subtle landscapes and implied horizons in her novels reveal her remapping of her geopolitical space.

Exile can create a double perspective, seeing the mother country first through the intensity of lived experience and then through the distance that comes with exile. Exiles are both inside and outside; "insiders" to the culture of the home country yet exiled from it; "outsiders" in the country of exile yet often living intimately within it. Thus the writer in exile is in a unique position to describe multiple international horizons of experience, and also to evoke with great power and tenderness the social, political, and geographic landscape of his or her imagined homeland. Ngugi's vision of Kenya, La Guma's re-creation of the townships of South Africa, and Head's evocative tales of Botswana reveal the power of exilic writing.

White writing in South Africa is also a kind of exilic writing. Doris Lessing has claimed that "all white African literature is the literature of exile: not from Europe, but from Africa" (Lessing, "Desert Child" 700). Lessing suggests that white writers in Africa are not able to identify themselves as citizens of their "home countries" in Europe, but find it difficult to claim the landscape of Africa for themselves. J.M. Coetzee asserts that alienation from the African landscape is widespread in white writing: "In the words he throws out to the landscape, in the echoes he listens for, [the poet] is seeking a dialogue with Africa, a reciprocity with Africa, that will allow him an identity better than that of visitor, stranger, transient" (Coetzee, *White Writing* 8). In Chapter 6, I explore this alienation in the works of André Brink, Nadine Gordimer, and Coetzee.

Displacement and exile disrupt the categories of native and immigrant. Is Bessie Head an immigrant writer because she was born in South Africa and wrote in Botswana? Is all of Ngugi's work part of Kenyan national literature, despite being written partially in exile? Do all writers born in a country belong to that national literature? Can one choose one's nation? For many of the writers in this study, their nationality, place of birth, and place of residence are not identical, creating hybrid, international texts. Even writers who never leave their home country may find their literary influences elsewhere: "We are inescapably international writers at a time when the novel has never been a more international form" (Rushdie 20). The description of landscape is complicated by the traces of these international perspectives.

RELIGION

Indigenous African religions often link a people to a specific place. Ife, in Nigeria, proudly proclaims itself to be "the cradle of the Yoruba race"; Kirinyaga

(Mount Kenya) is where God lives in the Gikuyu tradition. Even more than this, however, indigenous religions create complex cartographies of the physical and spiritual world. Gods, spirits, human communities, animals, and plants all inhabit the same universe, and small events may have cosmological significance. In discussing African drama, Soyinka states:

> The stage, the ritual arena of confrontation, came to represent the symbolic chthonic space and the presence of the challenger within it is the earliest physical expression of man's fearful awareness of the cosmic context of his existence. (Soyinka, *Myth, Literature and the African World* 3)

Ritual Yoruba drama doesn't merely represent, but recreates, man's efforts to harmonize with his physical and spiritual environment. A successful performance is one that restores the harmony among the physical, social, and spiritual realms. Traditional African religions create a spatio-temporal world which extends far beyond the limits of mere physical reality.

Christianity's influences on Africa have been manifold. Christian missionaries initially brought with them much the same message as imperialism, holding up as an ideal the values and morals of Christian Europe. Their map of the world was Eurocentric; Africans "lived in darkness," at the periphery of the known, Christian, world. Yet Christianity also has the potential to create alternative geographies. The Catholic Church may look to Rome as the center of the church, but political boundaries are less important than vertically imagined boundaries between earth, heaven, and hell. Christianity supplies both a historical trajectory, from the beginning to the end of the world, and also a competing atemporal vision: from the perspective of eternity, every moment is as important as any other. Further, Christians in fundamentalist sects are encouraged to read the world as a manifestation of God's will, a belief Soyinka explores in *Aké*. All of these beliefs affect attitudes towards landscape, boundaries, and horizons.

In most of Africa, Islam has an even longer history than Christianity. Islamic law provides an interpretive framework which defines one's interaction with the exterior landscape, such as the division of the day by the five periods of prayer and the seclusion of women. The ultimate goal of Islam, however, is to see this world as transitory, illusory. The real world is eternal and spiritual; the physical world is merely the world of appearance. In Chapter 3, I discuss the impact of Islam on landscape in Cheikh Hamidou Kane's *Ambiguous Adventure*.

While each of these religions has its own specific beliefs and practices, each provides a temporal horizon within which existence in the physical world is only a part of human experience. The landscape may be the arena of spiritual conflict, or only a temporary location for an essentially spiritual being. In each case, the physical world is only a partial, even possibly illusory, vision of reality.

CONCLUSION

Judith Butler's *Bodies That Matter* provides a persuasive analysis of power in Western culture, especially the power of the dominant discourse. Butler's analysis works through an analogy with juridical authority. Her deconstructive reading of juridical power emphasizes that juridical authority relies, not on prior authority, but on citation itself: "Prior authority proves to be *derived from* the contemporary instance of its citation" (Butler 109). Each citation is a reassertion of the primacy of juridical power. Yet, in the process of articulating its authority, "the law provides *the discursive occasion* for a resistance, a resignification, and potential self-subversion of that law" (Butler 109; author's italics). African authors writing in English are confronted with the task of reclaiming an Africa which has been claimed, controlled and dominated by a discourse of power from Europe and America, a discourse which until recently excluded African voices. Furthermore, this European discourse is only one of the powerful interpretive systems which influence the landscapes and horizons of African literature in English. Islam, Christianity, nationalism, and precolonial systems of authority have all had their impact on the discourse of African literature, and have been inscribed on the landscapes of African fiction. Yet African writers also have been able to use these dominant discourses to question and even to deconstruct their power, using, in Butler's terms, the moment of citation as a moment of resistance and resignification. In the following chapters, I explore how African writers have rewritten the African landscape, relocating their characters within local landscapes and national and global horizons which reflect their resistance to and their resignification and subversion of dominant discourses about Africa. Far from being a minor aspect of African literature, African landscapes provide a conceptual framework for the interpretation of African fiction.

NOTES

1. Henry Louis Gates' definition of Signifyin(g) is relevant here: "Signifyin(g) is black double-voicedness; because it always entails formal revision and an intertextual relation . . . I find it an ideal metaphor for black literary criticism, for the formal manner in which texts seem concerned to address their antecedents" (Gates 51); Signifyin(g) also refers to the way black African Americans signify upon white language and literature: "the black vernacular tradition created a homonymic pun of the profoundest sort, thereby marking its sense of difference from the rest of the English community of speakers. Their complex act of language Signifies upon both formal language use and its conventions" (Gates 47). What I am claiming here is that African writers evoke their own sets of antecedents and contemporary references, creating a specific intertextual matrix within which their own text signifies. As Judith Butler notes in *Bodies That Matter*, citations create and affirm their own precedents; this is particularly true for a literary text, which calls into being through allusion, repetition, inclusion, and opposition the texts by which and against which it defines itself.

2. In his description of J. P. Clark's poetry Adrian Roscoe does discuss Clark's use of "the details of physical Africa and the natural phenomena that inform it" (Roscoe, *Mother Is Gold* 36). Even though he introduces this discussion as an example of a new interest in landscape (Roscoe, *Mother Is Gold* 36), Roscoe proceeds to analyze it as "setting," and "the local scene," finally admiring Clark for illustrating "how an African poet . . . can work with a local theme and yet do so in a style which echoes the metropolitan tradition" (Roscoe, *Mother Is Gold* 38-39). Despite his admiration for Clark's work, Roscoe's reference to the "metropolitan tradition" and his

slippage in language from "landscape" to "local theme" reveal the persistence of a European standard which *defines* African literary techniques as lesser versions of Western techniques; the best that African writers can accomplish, in this view, is to imitate the masters well.

3. There are difficulties, however, with Bhabha's position.   Bhabha claims that "Once the liminality of the nation-space is established. . . .   the national subject splits in the ethnographic perspective of culture's contemporaneity and provides both a theoretical position and a narrative authority for marginal voices or minority discourse" (Bhabha 301).   The liminality of the nation-space, however, is what is constantly denied or repressed by the narrative of nationalism; its claim is to represent the (unified) whole.   Liminality can't be *established*; it is forever contested.   And this contestation aims precisely at avoiding the emergence of the marginal.   Thus the opening up of the nation-space seems predicated on a utopian moment—an acknowledgment by all parties of the plurality of the nation-space.

4. In "Yeats and Decolonization," liberation is not well-defined. Said returns to the discussion of liberation in *Culture and Imperialism*, once again seeing in Fanon a liberationist idea beyond nationalism. Liberation ideally would link struggles in the colonies to resistance movements within the metropole, creating a new, non-Eurocentric universalism that reaches beyond nationalism: "Fanon wants somehow to bind the European as well as the native together in a new non-adversarial community of awareness and anti-imperialism" (Said 274). Said provides a few characteristics of liberation: it is a "process" (274); it is "anti-identitarian" (274) and "anti-authoritarian" (278). Finding the source for this idea in the "poetic and visionary suggestions" (274) of Fanon's prose, Said provides only a sketchy account of what liberation might encompass as a political movement.

5. Homi K. Bhabha discusses Julia Kristeva's *Women's Time* and celebrates her "redefinition of the nation as a space for the emergence of feminist political and psychic identifications" (Bhabha 303), but he fails to take into account the preexisting feminist dialogue about the problematic relationship between women and the state. This failure limits his discussion of gender and nation; as I claim here, women, like Bhabha's migrants, can be seen as irreducibly plural players on the international scene, displacing and questioning the narratives of nationalism.

Chapter 1

Ngugi wa Thiong'o's Visions
of Africa

I was living in a village and also in a colonial situation.
— Ngugi, *Homecoming* 48

It has been said that Africans have no interest in landscape (Roscoe, *Uhuru's Fire* 177-78). If, however, as I have been suggesting, landscape is best understood as the description of the land and its role in the cultural, economic and spiritual life of the community, it immediately becomes clear that landscape is an essential part of African history and literature. Throughout the African novel, concerns about land use, ownership, spiritual values, nationalism, and pan-Africanism are reflected in the description of the land. In the Gikuyu writer Ngugi wa Thiong'o's work, the community's relationship to the land is of fundamental importance.[1]

Ngugi's descriptions of landscape are shaped by some specific circumstances of Kenyan history: the centrality of land in the Gikuyu worldview, the forced removals from the White Highlands, the Mau Mau independence movement, and post-independence disillusionment. Ngugi himself has insisted on the connection between particular historical events and literature:

Literature does not grow or develop in a vacuum; it is given impetus, shape, direction and even area of concern by social, political and economic forces in a particular society. (Ngugi *Homecoming* xv)

In analyzing the description of landscape in Ngugi's novels, I want to do more than show his mastery of a Western technique; Ngugi's works reevaluate the importance of landscape, integrating geography with his characters' cultural environment, religious beliefs and economic system.

Land is central to Gikuyu spiritual, cultural and economic practices:

To anyone who wants to understand Gikuyu problems, nothing is more important than a correct grasp of the question of land tenure. For it is the key to the people's life; it secures for them that peaceful tillage of the soil which supplies their material needs and enables them to perform their magic and traditional ceremonies in undisturbed serenity, facing Mount Kenya. (Kenyatta xxi)

Kenyatta's study of Gikuyu culture shows that the Gikuyu see land as connecting them to God and to their ancestors, as well as to the village community. In the Gikuyu myth of creation, the land was given to them by God; in addition, "Communion with the ancestral spirits is perpetuated through contact with the soil in which the ancestors of the tribe lie buried. The Gikuyu consider the earth as the 'mother' of the tribe. . . . Thus the earth is the most sacred thing above all that dwell in or on it" (Kenyatta 21). Ngugi's descriptions of land in his early novels incorporate these traditional Gikuyu beliefs about their land.

Colonialism caused catastrophic disruption in Gikuyu society. Not only were the Gikuyu forcibly brought under British colonial rule; the Gikuyu lands, particularly the area known as the White Highlands, were seen as especially suited for Europeans, because of the similarity between their climate and Europe's:

[A] point which is often overlooked is that regions most favoured by Europeans may be those least suited to Africans. Europeans instinctively select a country where the climate, vegetation and temperature most resemble those of the cold north. Natives, on the whole, thrive best in hotter, lower, wetter places. (Huxley, *White Man's Country* vol. 1 72)

In addition to this suggestion that there was a kind of racial affinity that justified the annexation of the Highlands, Huxley and others also claimed that the Gikuyu were not doing anything with the land: "To us, that was remarkable: they had not aspired to recreate or tame the country and to bring it under their control" (Huxley, *Flame Trees of Thika* 45). Throughout colonial African literature, there runs the theme that the land belongs to the people who would develop it, based loosely on the Biblical notion of the good steward. The good stewardship of the Gikuyu, and the environmental value of fallow land, was not yet appreciated by the British.

The British colonists then developed a legal argument justifying the appropriation of land:

The Europeans [misinterpreted Gikuyu land tenure] by saying that the land was under the communal or tribal ownership, and as such the land must be *mali ya serikali*, which means Government property. Having coined this new terminology of land tenure, the British Government began to drive away the original owners of the land. (Kenyatta 26)

Thus by a sleight of hand, communal land became the property of the Crown.

In actuality, the open land the Europeans saw in the Highlands was used as pasture-land and woodlands, and also represented future village sites, as populations expanded and farming plots became exhausted. By relocating whole villages as the soil gave out, the Gikuyu were able to design a sustainable agriculture; with the coming of permanent ownership of the land and a growing population, however, they were no longer able to move to open land, and their plots became poor and subdivided.

The Mau Mau uprising in Kenya in the 1950s was a crucial event not only in Kenyan history but also in Ngugi's personal development. His older brother, Wallace Mwangi, was a freedom fighter (Gurr 101). While Mau Mau was strongest among the Gikuyu, it was a national movement that united the Kenyan people: "Through Mau Mau, they organized themselves, in the villages, and in the towns, their vision going beyond the narrow confines of the tribe" (Ngugi *Homecoming* 12). Ngugi's political philosophy was strongly influenced by Marxism, but at the same time he felt that he was articulating a nationalist and socialist vision that was essentially African, not Western: "My thesis, when we come to today's Africa, is then very simple: a completely socialized economy, collectively owned and controlled by the people, is necessary for a national culture" (Ngugi *Homecoming* 13). Although Ngugi's early novels emphasize the relation of a specifically Gikuyu culture to the land, all his works also articulate a national and socialist vision of Kenya.

Ngugi grew up in a small village; he was sent to boarding school to get a British-style education, and later studied at Makerere and Leeds universities. His first three novels, *The River Between, Weep Not, Child*, and *A Grain of Wheat* were written in Uganda and England; *Petals of Blood* "was drafted in the USA and completed in the USSR" (Gurr 17). The traces of this history are apparent in the Western form and techniques used in these early novels. By examining the changes in the description of landscape in Ngugi's novels, and considering them as a response to colonial literature about Kenya and in connection with Ngugi's critique of the economic and political situation in Kenya, we can trace the development of his fiction from a limited acceptance of Western techniques of description to a rejection of these techniques as implying a view of nature that Ngugi no longer shares.

Ngugi's earliest novel (although it was published after *Weep Not, Child*) is *The River Between*. This novel opens with a sweeping description of the landscape:

The two ridges lay side by side. One was Kameno, the other was Makuyu. Between them was a valley. It was called the valley of life. Behind Kameno and Makuyu were many more valleys and ridges, lying without any discernable plan. They were like many sleeping lions which never woke. They just slept, the big deep sleep of their Creator.

A river flowed through the valley of life. If there had been no bush and no forest trees covering the slopes, you could have seen the river when you stood on top of either Kameno or Makuyu. Now you had to come down. Even then you could not see the whole extent of the river as it gracefully, and without any apparent haste, wound its way down the valley, like a snake. The river was called Honia, which meant cure, or bring-back-to-life. Honia river never dried: it seemed to possess a strong will to live, scorning droughts and weather changes. And it went on in the same way, never hurrying, never hesitating. People saw this and were happy. (*The River Between* 1)

The opening paragraphs can be compared to Western descriptions of landscape. The omniscient narrator supplies a bird's eye view of the landscape, and names the prominent features for us. The description is organized along the lines of a landscape painting: first we see the most prominent features, the two ridges, then the valley, and finally the background features are filled in. As in a novel by Dickens, Hardy or Lawrence, the landscape is used to foreshadow the conflicts in the novel: the river divides the two ridges, but could also be seen as a uniting force. Ngugi's use of the ambivalent term "between" in "between them was a valley" (and in the title of the novel) offers at least two interpretations; if people have something between them, it can join or divide them. Ngugi's use of personification in this passage stays within the limits of traditional realism: although the river is described as "possessing a strong will to live, scorning droughts and weather changes," the narrator distances himself from this description through the phrase "it seemed." As a final touch, Ngugi ends the paragraph with a reference to people, like the small figures, sometimes including a figure of the artist himself, included in a landscape painting to provide a sense of scale. An important difference here is that the figures are not of the artist, but of the community itself as collective onlookers: "People saw this and were happy."

When the landscape is looked at from inside the valley rather than from the air the foreshadowing of conflict is intensified: "When you stood in the valley, the two ridges. . . . became antagonists . . . they faced each other, like two rivals ready to come to blows in a life and death struggle for the leadership of this isolated region" (*The River Between* 1). The river divides rather than unites, marking the boundary between the two opposing sides (Christian and traditional villages). By placing these descriptions side by side, Ngugi leaves the "correctness" of either vision open; Waiyaki, the protagonist, must decide whether the Gikuyu are ready to be united, or are destined to be split into two camps. The choice of action is linked to the choice of perspective; if Waiyaki can persuade the villages to see themselves as united—part of the same community, the same valley—they will be able to overcome their differences, but if the river is seen as a boundary between the two rather than a unifying force, the social rift will be unbreakable.

Ngugi's description of the landscape is integrated with his development of action and character. Waiyaki's father, Chege, takes him to visit a place sacred to his clan, pointing out medicinal herbs along the way. Here, as Roscoe has observed, "the landscape, the forests and hills, are conspiring to unite father and son as they have united the Gikuyu nation for generations. We cannot understand the individual, social, and spiritual significance of either character outside their relation to the landscape" (*Uhuru's Fire* 178). Through this scene, we see

how Waiyaki is being educated in the connections between the Gikuyu community and nature, and specifically in the connections to this particular landscape,
where medicinal herbs grow, and where there are sacred sites. Ngugi's description of the community's relation to the land at the moment when colonialism,
through the arrival of Christian missionaries, was just beginning to make itself
felt, echoes Kenyatta's claims about the importance of land to the Gikuyu people: "These ancient hills and ridges were the heart and soul of the land. They
kept the tribes' magic and rituals, pure and intact" (*The River Between* 3).

Throughout the novel, the conflict between Christianity and traditionalism
is seen as threatening the people's connection to the land. In one scene,
Muthoni, the daughter of a minister, reveals to her sister Nyambura that she
wants to be circumcised and become "a real woman, knowing all the ways of
the hills and ridges" (*The River Between* 29). Nyambura is shocked by
Muthoni's decision, as it is against the principles of their church:

For a second Nyambura sat as if her thoughts, her feelings, her very being had been
paralysed. She could not speak. The announcement was too sudden and too stupefy-
ing. How could she believe what she had heard came from Muthoni's mouth? She
looked at the river, at the slightly swaying bulrushes lining the banks, and then beyond. Nothing moved on the huge cattle road that wound through the forest towards
Kameno. The yellowish streaks of morning light diffused through the forest, producing long shadows on the cattle path. The insects in the forest kept up an incessant
sound which mingled with the noise of falling water farther down the valley. They
helped to intensify the silence, created by Muthoni's statement.[2] (*The River Between*
28)

Female circumcision was (and continues to be) the cause of one of the crucial
conflicts between Christians and traditionalists: to Christians it is barbaric, but
without it, a woman cannot be initiated into her clan. That Muthoni, the daughter of a minister, would choose to be circumcised is extremely shocking, and it
has stunned her sister into silence. Yet Muthoni's description of her decision
shows that she sees this action as the only way to have an authentic connection
to the "hills and ridges." On the other hand, when Nyambura reaches out to the
landscape to reassure herself and support her Christian beliefs, she receives nothing: the insects' noise "helped to intensify the silence" and "nothing moved."
Ngugi's description clearly intimates that Christianity detaches the individual
from the landscape, both through the loss of traditional initiation rites which
would connect the individual to the clan and to the land, and through the loss of
traditional interpretations of the landscape—for Nyambura, the symbolic significance of the land in the Gikuyu culture has been lost. The land is silent.

In *The River Between*, the colonialists have not yet moved into the hills.
Their influence is felt through the Christian school in a nearby town, and their
political and economic power is known only through descriptions of their houses
and through the tax gatherers. Yet Waiyaki, the protagonist, senses what is to
come:

And still it rained, with the little streams gathering and joining together.   He saw
what they were doing—
     Carrying away the soil.
     Corroding, eating away the earth.
     Stealing the land.
And that was the cry, the cry on every ridge. Perhaps the sleeping lions would sleep
no more, for they were all crying, crying for the soil. The earth was important to the
tribe. (*The River Between* 76)

The "sleeping lions" are the valleys and ridges in Ngugi's initial description of
the landscape; the implication that they might wake now and challenge the destruction of the land foreshadows the revolutionary movement of Mau Mau in
Kenya. Waiyaki explicitly connects the irresistible erosion of the land with the
white settlers: "That was why Kinuthia and others like him feared the encroach-
ment of the white man" (*The River Between* 76). This coming threat emphasizes
the importance of Waiyaki's quest to unify the two villages; without unification,
both villages will be washed away by the erosion caused by the white settlers.
     Near the end of the novel, Ngugi again foreshadows the coming of Mau
Mau: "suddenly the people who stood on the hills or up the slope saw big yel-
low flames emanated by the setting sun. The flames seemed near and far and the
trees and the country were caught in the flames. They feared" (*The River Between*
166). Ngugi's image of the flames of the sunset suggests that the Mau Mau
uprising which it portends was a natural, even inevitable, phenomenon.
     Throughout the novel, the river Honia is a symbol of life, power and unifi-
cation. In this image, Ngugi draws on the importance of the river in traditional
life, as a source of water, and as a source of spiritual renewal. Even Christianity
is included in the landscape through the Biblical language used to represent the
river's song: "And Honia river went on flowing through the valley of life,
throbbing, murmuring an unknown song. *They shall not hurt nor destroy in all
my holy mountains, for the earth shall be full of the knowledge of the Lord, as
the waters cover the sea*" (*The River Between*, author's italics, 173). The river's
warning is unheeded by the people of Kameno: they reject their teacher, because
he preaches unification with the Christians of Makuyu. With the betrayal of
Waiyaki by the people of Kameno, it would seem that the hope of unification
has been lost forever, but Ngugi closes the novel with a final image of the river:
"Honia river went on flowing between them, down through the valley of life, its
beat rising above the dark stillness, reaching into the heart of the people of
Makuyu and Kameno" (175). The river's unifying presence implies that there is
still some possibility for change in Kenya.   Charles Nnolim, in his essay
"Background Setting: Key to the Structure of Ngugi's *The River Between*," sees
this as a tragic ending: "Ngugi seems to look on Honia River as symbolizing
the continued and eternal strife between the Makuyu and Kameno tribesman"
(Nnolim 138). However, in "Kenya: The Two Rifts" Ngugi uses a similar image: "Kenya is potentially a great country. . . . The different springs in every
tribe and race can and should be channelled to flow together in a national stream
from which all may draw" (*Homecoming* 24). In opposition to the eroding

forces of colonialism, Ngugi claims that nationalism and socialism are life-giving, unifying forces. Thus, although Waiyaki, the "middle figure" in between the two ridges, is unable to find a resolution, the Honia river's ability to flow into the heart of the people in both villages implies that there is still the possibility of unification and social change in Kenya.

Early critics of Ngugi's fiction noted his use of landscape as an integral part of *The River Between*. Ime Ikiddeh saw the Honia River as a symbol of the inherent unity of the two communities; the division between them is an "unnatural struggle" (Ikiddeh 5). In some Western interpretations of the novel, however, the description of landscape became a point of contention as to whether the novel was borrowing Western conventions of description or was revealing a uniquely African consciousness. In the first group was C. B. Robson, who linked Ngugi's description of landscape with D. H. Lawrence's and universalized the Kenyan struggle for independence in the novel: "Even his attempt to form a 'new retrospect,' of the clash with Europe, is conveyed as part of man's struggle to come to terms with the implications of his own momentum" (Robson 129). On the other side was Gerald Moore, who saw African writers in general as expressing a unity of nature that was lost to the West:

What seems to be involved is a complete identification of the poet with the constituent features of the landscape around him. He does not so much inhabit this landscape as become inhabited by it . . . . Western man simply cannot fuse himself back into a nature which he has deliberately set apart from himself in order to master it (Moore "The Negro Poet and his Landscape" 151).

Yet either way, whether these Western critics praise African writers for their continuity with Western traditions or for their alterity, the center of the discourse is the use of these literatures for a Western audience. Chris Wanjala, in *The Season of Harvest: A Literary Discussion* criticizes Moore's position, which "implies a homeliness of a writer in an environment of primeval innocence (Garden of Eden?) and bliss":

Such a society does not exist here in East Africa today. He [Moore] refers the writer's consciousness only to place and disregards the history of the forming nations of East Africa, and the connection of Ngugi's writings to the pre-independence nationalism in Kenya. (Wanjala 53-54)

The same criticism can be made of Robson's interpretation of the novel: by "elevating" the issue in the novel to a universal crisis of modern man, Robson elides the significance of the novel as a critique of Western colonialism and capitalism. Wanjala asserts that Ngugi's purpose is to portray "the destruction that inhered in colonialism and to evoke the need for a renewal and a rebirth of African cultural and economic institutions that help the African to be at home in his society and in his physical environment" (Wanjala 70). Thus in *The River Between*, Honia River is a representation of the potential for renewal in the two communities.

Ngugi's use of landscape in *The River Between* shares similarities with early works by other African authors, such as Chinua Achebe's *Things Fall Apart*. In each of these, the author uses some Western techniques and has an orientation towards a Western audience. Europeans had been claiming for years that Africa was the dark continent; Hegel called it "the land of childhood, which lying beyond the day of self-conscious history, is enveloped in the dark mantle of Night" (Hegel 91). In response, early African writers tended to produce novels proclaiming the humanity and cultural achievements of Africans—to show that Africa had a rich and complex history before the arrival of the white man. These early novels are intended for a Western as well as an African audience.

After their early novels, however, the careers of Ngugi and Achebe moved in different directions, as Achebe continued to claim that English can be African, while Ngugi began to write in Gikuyu. Ngugi puts into practice his own beliefs: "African literature can only be written in African languages" (*Decolonizing the Mind* 27). This policy is an adjunct to his Afrocentric vision: "The aim, in short, should be to orientate ourselves towards placing Kenya, East Africa, and then Africa in the centre" (*Homecoming* 146).

Even in *The River Between* there are elements of this vision: the novel centers on the Gikuyu people, and the colonists are only on the fringes of the Gikuyu world. Ngugi carefully depicts the land-centered consciousness of the Gikuyu, and uses their symbolic system to describe and interpret the significance of the landscape. However, the form of the novel is Westernized, and Ngugi gradually turns from this style to develop an African-centered approach not only to the content, but also to the structure of his novels.

Between the publication of *A Grain of Wheat* (1968) and *Petals of Blood* (1977), Ngugi published a collection of nonfiction essays, *Homecoming* (1972), which describe his positions on colonialism, nationalism, capitalism, and post-independence corruption in Africa. The essays are focused on the present and the future, rather than the past described in his early novels. Significantly, he rejects the romanticism of the past typical of the Negritude poets:

. . . the African writer was in danger of becoming too fascinated by the yesterday of his people and forgetting the present. Involved as he was in correcting his disfigured past, he forgot that his society was no longer peasant, with common ownership of means of production, with communal celebration of joy and victory, communal sharing of sorrow and bereavement; his society was no longer organized on egalitarian principles. (*Homecoming* 44)

Ngugi claims that there are no longer any tribes in Africa: "the economic and social forces that gave rise to various nations in pre-colonial Africa have collapsed" (xvii). In this new world, he urges Africans to look, not to the past, but to the future: "For we are all involved in a common problem: how best to build a true communal home for all Africans. Then all the black people, all the African masses can truthfully say: we have come home" (xix). The Marxist ideology and African-centered consciousness of *Homecoming* form the ideological context of *Petals of Blood*.

In *Petals of Blood*, Ngugi moves from the primarily aesthetic and spiritual connection to the land evident in his early novels to an explicitly political and economic relationship between the worker and the land. Instead of identifying characters as Gikuyu or Maasai, he calls them tillers, peasants and herdsmen (Gurr 109), thus de-emphasizing the role of specific cultures in creating and maintaining the people's relationship to their environment. Rather, the cycles of human life are seen as intricately interwoven with the cycles of production:

The peasant farmers of Ilmorog now went into the fields to idly earth up crops that no longer needed the extra earth, or to merely pull out the odd weed. Thistles, marigolds and forget-me-nots would stick to their clothes, and they would now laugh and tell jokes and stories as they waited for the crops to ripen. (*Petals of Blood* 32).

The happiness and idleness of the peasant farmers is clearly linked to the time of year.

Earlier religious attitudes are rejected here:

A donkey has no influence on the weather. No animal or man can change the laws of nature. But people can use the laws of nature. The magic we should be getting is this: the one which will make this land so yield in times of rain that we can keep aside a few grains for when it shines ... Let us rather look to ourselves to see what we can do to save us from the drought. The labour of our hands is the magic and wealth that will change our world and end all droughts from our earth. (*Petals of Blood* 115)

While Karega, the protagonist, shares his community's vision of the land as belonging to the people as a whole, he rejects the "magical" beliefs of the community in favor of a socialist approach which relies on labor and communal action rather than on ancestral ties to preserve the productiveness of the land. Ngugi even refigures the Gikuyu's reverence for ancestral spirits associated with the land through his revolutionary perspective: listening to stories of the Mau Mau, Karega becomes "aware of a new relationship to the ground on which they trod ... everything on the plains had been hallowed by the feet of those who had fought and died that Kenya might be free: wasn't there something, a spirit of those people in them too?" (*Petals of Blood* 143).

Godfrey Munira in *Petals of Blood* is a schoolteacher, like Waiyaki in *The River Between*. While Waiyaki was at the center of his people's conflict between Christianity and traditional culture, Munira is portrayed as an outsider, not only because he was not born in Ilmorog, but also because he does not work on the land: "Munira did not take part in such talk: he felt an outsider to [the peasants'] involvement with both the land and what they called 'things of blood' ... he seemed doomed to roam this world, a stranger" (*Petals of Blood* 18).

The figure of Munira, the Western-educated schoolteacher, serves as an indictment of a Western attitude toward nature. Munira's aesthetic appreciation of nature is divorced from practicalities: "He would watch the peasants in the fields going through the motions of working but really waiting for the rains, and he would vaguely feel with them in their anxieties over the weather. But the sun was nice and warm on his skin" (*Petals of Blood* 20). His attitude is similar to the traditional Western pastoral depiction of rural life, which elevated the picturesque qualities of rural scenes but tended to overlook the poverty of the rural people and their struggles to survive on marginal land. Munira shies away from anything beyond conventional Western aesthetic values. While on a nature walk, one of Munira's students says "Look. A flower with petals of blood." Munira immediately corrects him: "There is no color called blood. What you mean is that it is red" (21). Just as he felt outside the "things of blood" the farmers discuss, Munira here avoids the implications of "petals of blood." Only towards the end of the novel is Munira able to accept this image: after setting fire to a whorehouse, Munira

stood on the hill and watched the whorehouse burn, the tongues of flame from the four corners forming petals of blood, making a twilight of the dark sky. He, Munira, had willed and acted, and he felt, as he knelt down to pray, that he was no longer an outsider, for he had finally affirmed his oneness with the Law. (*Petals of Blood* 333)

Action imbues the petals of blood with meaning. In the earlier scene, however, the children's questions about the relationships of man to nature only irritate him: "Man . . . law . . . God . . . nature [sic]; he had never thought deeply about these things, and he swore that he would never again take the children to the fields" (*Petals of Blood* 22).

Munira is an intruder in the community, a man who fails to establish any lasting ties. He is the image of the Western-educated African, aspiring to Western ideals but left out of the real centers of power. He fantasizes about being "master" of Ilmorog: "he came to feel as if Ilmorog was his personal possession . . . he felt as if the whole of Ilmorog had put on a vast flower-patterned cloth to greet its lord and master" (*Petals of Blood* 21). The language Munira uses, that of owner, master, and lord reveals his desire for power and control; it is the language of the colonial masters. Yet Munira's fantasies about nature do not lead to any ties to the community or to a sense of belonging in Ilmorog, but only to frustration. Munira's alienation from the land represents the contradictions involved in a Kenyan accepting Western premises about nature, power and community: Ngugi implies that in an African context, these premises are irrelevant and futile.

Karega, the hero of the novel, is also a schoolteacher, but he is able to see the connection of the land to the labor of the people. In addition, he represents Ngugi's desire to create an Afrocentric worldview. Karega asks, "How could he enlarge [the schoolchildren's] consciousness so that they could see themselves, Ilmorog and Kenya as part of a larger whole, a larger territory containing the history of African people and their struggles?" (*Petals of Blood* 109). This opinion is echoed later by the narrator, who comments that "the weakness of the resistance lay not in the lack of will or determination or weapons but in the African people's toleration of being divided into regions and tongues and dialects according to the wishes of former masters" (262). Africans, by accepting a

Western-oriented worldview, accepted also the arbitrary divisions created by the colonial powers and then maintained by those in power. A new image of a united Africa would be, quite literally, revolutionary.

In *Homecoming*, Ngugi claimed that "Now there are only two tribes left in Africa: the 'haves' and the 'have nots'" (*Homecoming* xvii). In *Petals of Blood* the "haves" are the Europeanized blacks who work for foreign companies: "the new owners, master-servants of bank power, money and cunning" (*Petals of Blood* 280). Ilmorog is divided into two parts—a wealthy residential area, and the shanty town of the workers. This rift is not illustrated or supported by any split in the natural landscape—there is no river between them—which emphasizes the unnatural nature of the division. The only differences are in the manmade landscape, in which Ngugi juxtaposes "Cape Town" whose luxuries simulate the power and privilege of its namesake, with the open sewers and mud shanties of the "New Jerusalem" (whose hopes must lie in the future). Karega finally blames the system of private ownership for the destruction of the land:

Why, anyway, should soil, any soil, which after all was what was Kenya, be owned by an individual? Kenya, the soil, was the people's common shamba, and there was no way it could be right for a few, or a section, or a single nationality, to inherit for their sole use what was communal. (*Petals of Blood* 302)

Ngugi has moved from a description of a single people's connection with its ancestral homeland to a national, even pan-African, perspective. In the process, he has described how people's relationships to the land, and by extension, to Kenya and to Africa, are mediated by their cultural, racial, and economic situation. Ngugi moves away from traditional descriptions of landscape, as in the opening of *The River Between*, towards descriptions that expose these mediating factors. For Ngugi, peasants have the most authentic experience of the land, in that their toil gives them a connection to the landscape which is not based on ownership or aesthetic distance, but this connection must be supplemented by teachers like Karega who can provide a vision of Kenyan and African unity. This vision will only become a reality through the masses' struggle against capitalism:

Imperialism: capitalism: landlords: earthworms. A system that bred hordes of round-bellied jiggers and bedbugs with parasitism and cannibalism as the highest goal in society. . . . The system and its gods and its angels had to be fought consciously, consistently and resolutely by all the working people! (*Petals of Blood* 344)

After *Petals of Blood*, Ngugi coauthored a play in Gikuyu, *Ngaahika Ndeenda*. The play was staged in his home town, Limuru, and was acted by the *wananchi*, or peasants, of the area. By writing in Gikuyu, and choosing the theater over the novel, Ngugi was identifying himself with the African masses, trying to put into practice his idea of cultural and political commitment. As a result, he was detained under the Public Security Act of Kenya in December 1977. After his release, in December 1978, Ngugi said: "*Ngaahika Ndeenda* showed me the road along which I should have been travelling all these past seventeen years of my writing career" (Ngugi, "Ngugi still bitter over his detention" 32). Since that time, Ngugi has been the leading proponent of writing in African languages.

The use of a foreign language creates a rift between the text and the author. Ngugi, by the time he wrote *Petals of Blood*, had already rejected Western techniques of description as implying Western, not African, relations to the land; now he rejected the language of the West also. Ngugi's decision reflects his concern with the alienation of the African from his own culture through the acceptance of Western culture and technology; Ngugi claims that "Literature published in African languages will have to be meaningful to the masses and therefore much closer to the realities of their situation" (Ngugi "On Writing in Gikuyu" 151).

In *Devil on the Cross*, Ngugi writes in Gikuyu from a Gikuyu perspective. The narrator of the story is a *gicaandi* singer, a traditional storyteller. He punctuates his narrative with African proverbs: "the forest of the heart is never cleared of all its trees" (7); "Aping others cost the frog its buttocks" (12). These proverbs connect the narrative with the oral tradition. They also provide a rhythm to the narrative development, and a logic for conversations between characters different from that of traditional Western narratives. Proverbs in African orature "attract the imagination of the listeners by the poetic effectiveness of their expression and . . . lend authority and weight to argument because they are generally recognized as eternal truths" (Okpewho 231). In Ngugi's novel, this strategy is used in conversations, as characters argue over the problems of modern Kenya. For example, Muturi argues for socialism in Kenya by referring to Gikuyu proverbs: "Humanity is in turn born of many hands working together, for, as Gikuyu once said, a single finger cannot kill a louse; a single log cannot make a fire last through the night" (*Devil on the Cross* 52). In another passage, a corrupt businessman also uses proverbs to support his own actions. Not all of the proverbs are traditional; some are taken from contemporary experience: "Money can flatten mountains" (117). Through these proverbs, Ngugi directs his narrative to a Gikuyu audience. At the same time, he shows that traditional wisdom alone is not enough to guide contemporary African society; it can be called upon to support both African socialism and neocolonial corruption. Readers must decide for themselves which argument is more persuasive.

In a similar manner, Ngugi incorporates Christian rhetoric and imagery into the novel, beginning with the title, *Devil on the Cross*. Wariinga has a recurring dream in which the Devil, not Christ, gets down from the cross, mocking and oppressing the people of Kenya. In *Petals of Blood*, Ngugi had rejected Christianity, and accepted traditional wisdom only insofar as it described a communal, socialist society. In *Devil on the Cross*, however, Ngugi uses both traditional Gikuyu culture and Christianity as elements of contemporary Kenyan culture, and as sources for the rhetoric of his characters. Even the narrator, the *gicaandi* singer, describes a vision he has had in Biblical and apocalyptic terms: "And after seven days had passed, the Earth trembled, and lightning scored the sky with its brightness, and I was lifted up, and I was borne up to the rooftop of the house, and I was shown many things" (*Devil on the Cross* 8). As in the figure of the Devil on the cross, Biblical imagery is used to intensify Ngugi's own argument; the range of diction and symbolic structures has expanded considerably from the narrowly socialist rhetoric of *Petals of Blood*.

The *gicaandi* singer's story begins with a description of the alienation of a working-class woman in Nairobi. Fired from her job for refusing sexual advances, then rejected by her boyfriend, Jacinta Wariinga is thrown out of her apartment. All of these events make her lose her sense of perspective: "Instantly she felt dizzy. Nairobi—people, buildings, trees, motor cars, streets—began to swirl before her eyes" (*Devil on the Cross* 12). Without a home, a lover, or a job, Wariinga has no connection to her environment, and is alienated from it. Her dizziness is the result of the social and economic disruptions in her life.

Wariinga then takes a *matatu*, a van, from Nairobi to Ilmorog. During this trip, several characters discuss the problems of modern Kenya, symbolized by an upcoming "Devil's Feast" for "Modern Thieves and Robbers" in a cave in Ilmorog. The bus trip provides a transition between the real Kenyan city and Ngugi's fictional Ilmorog. Ilmorog can stand for all of Kenya, because the same people control the economy and the political structure everywhere in Kenya.

The division of Ilmorog into two sections, which was described in *Petals of Blood*, has become even more exaggerated. The rich live in "Golden Heights," which "contains the homes of the wealthy and the powerful. But do you call them homes or residences! Homes or sheer magnificence?" (*Devil on the Cross* 130). "New Jerusalem" has also gotten poorer: "The walls and the roofs of the shanties are made of strips of tin, old tarpaulin and polythene bags" (130).

In traditional Gikuyu stories, as in many African stories, ordinary and fantastic events take place side by side—the ordinary world and the spiritual universe are interconnected. In *Devil on the Cross* Ngugi utilizes this characteristic dimension of African literature for the first time in his fiction, going beyond the limits of Western realism. The best example of Ngugi's use of fantastic elements is the feast in the sumptuous cave for the "Modern Thieves and Robbers." They have transformed the cave into a huge hall, with chandeliers and luxurious furniture. In this environment, Kenyan businessmen try to outdo one another in stories of white collar thievery and corruption in order to win prizes from the International Organization of Thieves and Robbers. Here, Ngugi plays with Milton's description in *Paradise Lost* of the devils' first meeting in hell. The irony is that in Milton's version, the devils are ultimately powerless, subjected to God's will even in Hell, while the thieves and robbers in Ngugi's cave have enormous power in Kenya: only a revolution could stop them.

Another parallel is, of course, Plato's cave in *The Republic*, in which people are chained to a wall and watch the shadows of figures and other objects carried by unseen people. This parallel is underlined in Ngugi's novel when Wariinga steps out of the cave:

"Although I have just been in the full glare of electric lights, I feel as if I have lived in darkness all my life," Wariinga sighed, and then she added in a sing-song voice: "Praise the sun of God! Hail the light of God!"

"You should be singing praises to the light of our country," Gatuiria told her. (*Devil on the Cross* 128)

The electric lights, like the fire casting the shadows on the wall of Plato's cave, are artificial; the natural light of the sun, as in Plato's allegory, exposes the darkness of the cave. Wariinga's sing-song voice, as she praises God for this light, sounds childlike, a memorized chant. To Ngugi, this Christian response to the corruption of the people in the cave is mechanical and pointless, as Wariinga's sighs will not lead to real change. Gatuiria's claim that the light of truth is the light of the country, foreshadows the protests of the peasants, students and workers against the robbers in the cave.

Inside Plato's cave, the people who create plausible fictions about the meaning of the shadows on the wall are praised, while the one who, like Socrates, frees himself and seeks the light of the sun is despised. In Ngugi's novel, the businessmen/robbers in the cave create stories to convince the people that what they are doing is beneficial to the nation. As in Plato's cave, the stories that make the people praise the ones who keep them from discovering the truth are the worst evil. Ngugi's use of allusions to Western canonical texts emphasizes that the businessmen are operating within a Western context. They are practicing an unbridled Western capitalism, and, at the banquet, they are trying to impress their European masters.

There is a possibility for change. Wariinga and Gatuiria, wandering in the sunlight outside of the cave, enthusiastically sing a hymn to Kenya:

Hail, Mount Kenya!
Hail, our land.
Never without water or food or green fields! (*Devil on the Cross* 128)

Their love for each other is depicted as in harmony with the landscape: "The grass is a free bed given us by God, and the darkness is his blanket!" (241). As in the conclusion of *Petals of Blood*, the main characters decide to make a new beginning through their own efforts. This new beginning is a violent one: Wariinga discovers that Gatuiria's father was her first seducer, and she shoots him with a pistol. Gatuiria, the man who has been trying to write a new Kenyan opera, is at a loss: he stands looking after her, "hearing in his mind music that leads him nowhere" (*Devil on the Cross* 254). Wariinga strides into the future, "without once looking back" (254).

In *Devil on the Cross*, Ngugi champions women's rights in Kenya. He argues for the education of women, especially practical education: Wariinga trains to become an auto mechanic. Ngugi is particularly concerned about the treatment of women as the sexual possessions of men; he also deplores women's attempts to lighten their skin, straighten their hair, and follow the current fashions, and celebrates the beauty of African women who are strong and independent. Wariinga, at the conclusion of the novel, is clearly the committed revolutionary, while her lover Gatuiria hesitates, uncertain what path he will take.

At times, Ngugi's novel seems too full of speeches, as each character gives his or her own autobiography and either boasts about his or her prowess (the thieves and robbers) or argues for a revolution. In the landscape of the novel, however, Ngugi clearly broadens the horizons of his fiction, including surreal locations and exaggerated landscapes that transform his story into an allegorical and mythical tale. This strategy also aligns his work with the tradition of oral African narratives. Thus Ngugi has not only written *Devil on the Cross* in Gikuyu; he has also reinvented the style and form of his fiction.

Ngugi's most recent novel, *Matigari*, was published in Gikuyu in 1987. The novel is an allegory, a story of Everyman; as Ngugi says in "To the Reader/Listener:"

This story is imaginary.
The actions are imaginary.
The characters are imaginary.
The country is imaginary—it has no name even.
Reader/listener: may the story take place in the country of your choice! (*Matigari* ix)

Compared to his earlier works, *Matigari* has a simplified landscape and a streamlined narrative. Matigari ma Njiruungi (His name means "'the patriots who survived the bullets'—the patriots who survived the liberation war, and their political offspring" [trans. note 20]) has come out of the forests. He wanders through the countryside looking for his children and asking: "My friends! Can you tell me where a person could find truth and justice in this country?" (*Matigari* 72). Matigari's character represents everyone who toiled under the colonialists and fought in the war of independence; he says "I tended the estates that spread around the house for miles. . . . I worked all the machines and in all the industries, but it was Settler Williams who would take the profits" (21). Rumors grow that he is the Angel Gabriel, or the Second Coming of Christ, and the government and the police become anxious to hunt him down. In the end, they accomplish this, chasing him into a river while they ride after their hounds, as if he were a fox, but meanwhile the boy Muriuki, who now calls himself and his friends "the children of the patriots," has picked up Matigari's gun and sword. Matigari ma Njiruungi remains undefeated.

The landscape of the novel is presented sparingly, as in an oral tale. There is a fig tree, where Matigari hid his rifle, a house he wishes to reclaim as his own with the estates surrounding it, a village, a city, and the country. The house is sketchily described: "there on the top of the hill overlooking the whole country stood a huge house which seemed to stretch out for miles, as if, like the plantation itself, it had no beginning and no end" (*Matigari* 42). It represents the shelter, food and clothing which should be the result of the labor of the people, but which has been wrongly appropriated by those "who-reap-where-they-have-not-sown" (50). As Matigari talks to the current owners, the sun sets behind the house: "it had left behind a blood-red glow in the evening sky, lighting up the house, the gate and the road on which they stood" (47-48), foreshadowing the fire that will burn it down at the end of the story.

Matigari begins his journey by crossing the river and coming out of the forest. The forest was a haven for the freedom fighters in Kenya, protecting them from the British colonial soldiers. But when Matigari retreats to the forest to find the answer to his question, an old woman rebukes him: "My dear wanderer, you cannot find answers to your questions here where nobody lives. Truth and justice are to be found in people's actions" (*Matigari* 87). The wilderness can provide shelter, but it cannot provide answers. In a situation in which it would be tempting to use the wilderness as a symbol of spiritual renewal and dedication, Ngugi turns away from it, and seeks renewal within the community.

Within the novel, there are enough details of the past history of the country and the freedom fighters to clearly identify the location as Kenya. Yet in his introductory poem, Ngugi insists on the timelessness and placelessness of his story, connecting his narrative to traditional explanatory folktales: "Most tales of the explanatory kind assume a large prehistoric time scale within which the images can range more freely than may be allowed even in mythic legends" (Okpewho 204). Ngugi also implies that the reading of his story should be like listening to a storyteller: each retelling is a reliving, a reenactment of the story. In *Matigari*, this connection is particularly powerful: each reader/listener can ask him or herself if the patriots have returned, and where justice and truth can be found in the country. By reading, Ngugi's audience participates in the awakening of the country.

In "A Note on the English Edition," Ngugi relates some of the consequences of this blurring of fact and fiction:

By January 1987, intelligence reports had it that peasants in Central Kenya were whispering and talking about a man called Matigari who was roaming the whole country making demands about truth and justice. There were orders for his immediate arrest, but the police discovered that Matigari was only a fictional character in a book of the same name. In February 1987, the police raided all the bookshops and seized every copy of the novel. (*Matigari* viii)

The readers of the book gave life, at least temporarily, to Matigari, whom the police tried to arrest. Failing in this, they arrested the book: "Matigari, the fictional hero, and the novel, his only habitation, have been effectively banned in Kenya" (*Matigari* viii). In this short note, Ngugi shrinks the fictional landscape of the novel into the confines of the book, and then imagines both the book and Matigari as outcasts: "With the publication of this English edition, they have joined their author in exile" (*Matigari* viii). The place of this placeless, timeless book, is the place of exile.

This brings us to the poignant ironies of Ngugi's situation: passionately attached to the land of Kenya, he is in exile from it; committed to writing in Gikuyu, he publishes his novels in that language only to see them banned. The English language edition, translated not by Ngugi himself but by Wangui wa Goro, is to him an exiled version of his text, enclosed in a non-African language. Thus Ngugi is distanced from his own work, at least from the only version in print. The event of the novel's publication and the circumstances surrounding it become part of the interpretation of the novel; it is only through his fictional character, Matigari, that Ngugi can return to Kenya. The book's publication in Kenya had allowed the author's ideas to reappear in that country, and the landscape of the novel had allowed for the reappearance of heroes in Kenya. The banning of the novel reinforces and intensifies the author's own exile. The landscape of the novel, then, is not only the simplified allegorical landscape of the tale, but also the political landscape which places the author and the book in specific relations to the country, identifying Ngugi and his novel as both Kenyan and expatriate, part of and excluded from the land.

In this examination of Ngugi's fiction, we have seen Ngugi move away from the traditional Western techniques of landscape description used in *The River Between*, to a broadening of the concept of landscape to include the social and political environment surrounding the publication of the novel itself. The fictional and factual landscapes of *Matigari* influence and interpenetrate each other, creating a charged atmosphere that challenges the reader to go beyond a simple aesthetic appreciation of the novel and to engage the political landscape on his or her own terms. The intended audience of Ngugi's later fiction is more and more clearly Kenyan, and African, not Western. Ngugi's works reveal the importance of landscape in African fiction, and the development of his style shows the possibilities and pitfalls of incorporating African elements into a Western form. Ultimately, Ngugi chooses to model the form of the novel itself on the traditions of African orature. In *Matigari*, the subtle descriptions of the hills and valleys of Kenya have disappeared, but the symbolic and political landscapes stand out more clearly. In this way, Ngugi places his fiction squarely within the larger African political landscape, and outside the mainstream of the Western tradition.

NOTES

1. This chapter was published in *Research in African Literatures* 26:4 (Winter, 1995). I am grateful for their permission to republish it here. I presented an early version of this chapter at the 8th Conference of the Modern Languages Association of Nigeria, University of Nigeria in February, 1991. I am grateful for the helpful comments of my audience on the importance of oral traditions for an understanding of Ngugi's strategies and style.

2. Adrian Roscoe offers the following comment on this passage:

Muthoni's announcement is heard by 'the river' which neatly divides the landscape and the human community of the book . . . . Even 'the slightly swaying bulrushes' have their place in this scene, repeating a reed-in-the-tide image which J. P. Clark popularized as a symbol of cultural hesitation. Muthoni so far has been weak like this plant; but now by the waters of the Honia she has made a decision which will restore her to strength. (*Uhuru's Fire* 177)

Chapter 2

Mother Africa: African Women and the Land in West African Literature

Black woman, woman of Africa, O my mother, I am thinking of you.
—Camara Laye, *The African Child*

Camara Laye's epigraph moves effortlessly from the symbolic to the specific, from "woman of Africa" to "my mother." Mother, *The* Mother, Mother Africa: the ideal "woman of Africa" becomes, is, the ideal mother, and the speaker's longed-for mother is the emblem of all women. African womanhood has been characterized as "that glorified niche carved out of the birth-pangs that constitute every mother's everlasting joy" (Ojo-Ade 72). Womanhood, again, *is* motherhood; in this view, an African woman is not a complete woman, not a "woman of Africa" unless she is a mother. The emphasis on motherhood for African women has led to the creation of a "woman's space" in literature, meaning both a space for women's writing and a fictive space for female characters, which is both limited and potentially liberating. African women writers explore the geography, the boundaries, and contours of this space for African women.

During the height of négritude's ideological dominance, a simplified image of the African past became popular: a romantic Golden Age, when women knew their place and valued it. This image has been used to criticize and control women in contemporary African society: "the few women who . . . engage in politics are reminded by hecklers and friends that their rightful place is 'beside the three cooking stones with the children'" (Obbo 15). Yet this image of "traditional women" sadly misrepresents the multiplicity of women's roles in traditional African societies. As Margaret Jean Hay and Sharon Stichter have asserted,

In contrast to pre-colonial societies in many other parts of the world, women traditionally played a major role in food cultivation and trade, in addition to food preparation and child-rearing. In some, though not all, African societies, women enjoyed control over the fruits of their labor and wielded substantial political power. (Hay and Stichter ix)

Women had multiple roles, and were not limited to "the three cooking stones and the children." Further, the appeal to "tradition" implies an appeal to an unchanging, immutable past. Traditional African societies, however, are not so easily defined or discovered. Tradition itself, as V. Y. Mudimbe claims, should not be seen as a static concept: "tradition (*traditio*) means discontinuities through a dynamic continuation and possible conversion of *traditia* (legacies)" (Mudimbe 189). In traditional African societies, both men's and women's roles changed over time; the meaning of gender roles was not necessarily fixed and immutable.

One particularly significant role for women in some African societies is the ·role of the storyteller, the *griot* . Oladele Taiwo in *Female Novelists of Modern Africa* claims that in traditional societies, "Much attention is paid to the training of a girl so that she may be well brought up to transmit the cultural norms of the society to her children. In this way she helps to maintain the continuity of the ethnic group and the race" (Taiwo 2). Women, in this view, are only cultural transmitters, not creators; they are conduits for knowledge between adults (males) and children. In contrast to this, Obioma Nnaemeka notes the variety of women's oral storytelling strategies: "At work and at home, women weave personal experiences into solitary songs that often constitute personal statements. Women also use political songs, lampoons and abusive songs as forms of social control" (Nnaemeka 139). Women are both professional and nonprofessional performers, active participants "in the crafting, preservation and transmission of most forms of oral literature" (Nnaemeka 138). Taiwo's interpretation of women's role in storytelling restricts women's participation to transmission, omitting women's creative strategies in composing original songs and transforming oral narratives into personal or political commentary. Women, through storytelling, have the power to influence the perception of cultural beliefs and practices, and to emphasize their own values in the stories they hand down to their children.

Of course, not every precolonial African society offered manifold opportunities to women. It has been asserted, however, that in many cases it was the effect of outside influences, such as Islam, Christianity, and colonization, not precolonial African traditions, that restricted the roles and opportunities of women:

Some scholars (Boserup, 1970; Van Allen, 1974) suggest that the combination of capitalist exploitation and European ideas about appropriate economic and domestic roles for women all but destroyed the economic independence and traditional form of social authority exercised by African women in the pre-colonial era. (Hay and Stichter 10-11)

So it is possible that African men's appeal to woman's "traditional place" within the home is revelatory of their own unconscious acceptance of European ideals of womanhood and domesticity, combined with a simplistic image of the African past.

Even when women participated in nationalist movements in Africa, their participation did not necessarily result in changed attitudes towards women's roles. As Elleke Boehmer has said, "Figures of mothers of the nation are everywhere emblazoned but the presence of women in the nation is officially marginalised and generally ignored" (Boehmer 6). Boehmer explores how the discourse of nationalism iconizes women as mothers but refuses to recognize women's other contributions to the state. Boehmer argues that "the emergence of nationalism was characterized by a co-operation between patriarchies in the nation-state and in the household" (Boehmer 7). In Africa, male elites were already in place: "With a dominant male presence rooted in the state, it was predictable that a gender bias would persist in neo-colonial nationalisms well beyond the time of independence" (Boehmer 7). Thus nationalism did not bring with it equality for women, but tended to replicate colonial discourses about women. These historical circumstances restricted women's access to political power and public space.

AFRICAN MEN'S LITERATURE

In literature by African men, African women have often been portrayed as either idealized, traditional women (Okot p'Bitek's Lawino) or debased modern women, often prostitutes (Cyprian Ekwensi's Jagua Nana). The strength of traditional female characters, such as Lawino, comes from their identification with their families and their culture. Even Ngugi wa Thiong'o, in his early novel *The River Between*, portrays women as self-affirming only through their loyalty to tradition.

In *The River Between*, Muthoni, daughter of a village minister, struggles with the conflicting ideals of her people and her father's religion: according to one, she must undergo female circumcision to become a woman; according to the other, it is a defilement of her body. The struggle for supremacy between Christianity and Gikuyu traditions intersects in the female body, which then embodies the struggle for the power to define women, and femininity, in the African community. In Ngugi's novel, Muthoni's decision to undergo clitoridectomy is seen as a liberating, revolutionary act, and yet it is an act that requires the mutilation of her body. Women's space, women's choice, are restricted in either system; women are not expected, or allowed, to carve out a new space for themselves.[1]

Characters such as Jagua Nana, in contrast to the "good" traditional woman, serve as warnings to African women not to become too modern, too "Westernized": modernity for women is identified with immorality. Jagua Nana, the urban prostitute, is the symbol of modern, debased, African womanhood; Nana's return to the countryside at the end of the novel underlines this moral. Thus the risks for any African woman, including any African woman writer, in claiming the space of modernity for themselves are enormous—they, like Jagua

Nana, may be accused of forgetting their true identity, their high moral position as mothers of Africa, and prostituting themselves to Western ways.

AFRICAN WOMEN'S LITERATURE

African women writers are sensitive, perhaps to a fault, to the preexisting images of woman's space. Their preoccupation with motherhood and/or barrenness as *the* crucial element in women's lives, in novels such as *Efuru, The Joys of Motherhood, The Bride Price,* and *So Long A Letter* has led Obioma Nnaemeka to characterize these works as "motherhood literature." Elaine Savory Fido has identified the original "motherland" as the mother's *body*—that with which we identify, from which we learn to separate. The mother country is also the mother's cultural and national identity, which gives children their first social identity. Thus the mother is at the center of the motherland: "[she is] the one who is the starting point of all journeys and the point of reference for all destinations. . . . In a sense, we know that there is no homecoming unless mother is at the end of it" (Fido 330). Fido uses this definition to explore the painful separations of Buchi Emecheta, Bessie Head, and Jean Rhys, not only from their mother countries, but from their mothers, and she sees this pattern replicated in their fiction: "Ona's death makes the condition of mother-loss the crucial factor in Nnu Ego's difficult life, and thus is Emecheta's own estrangement from her mother also re-enacted" (Fido 342). Fido shows that women writers also may blur the distinctions between mother, The Mother and Mother Africa.

Within African women's literature, the equation of womanhood with motherhood is asserted, but it is also probed and questioned. African women writers explore the space of motherhood, sometimes exposing it as illusory (*The Joys of Motherhood*) or claiming it as a liberatory space for self-reflection and self-discovery (*So Long A Letter*). Ama Ata Aidoo's ambivalent attitude is typical: "Oh, being a mother! Traditionally, a woman is supposed to be nothing more valid than a mother. Sometimes one gets nervous of such total affirmation and total negation in relation to other roles that one has played. But I think that being a mother has been singularly enriching" (Aidoo 13).

In every novel in this chapter, the central character is a woman who is or becomes a mother. African women's literature, by centering stories on the experience of motherhood, shapes the African landscape from a woman's perspective, moving outward from the family, with mothers and children at the core of the novel. African women writers, through their focus on womanhood and motherhood, are testing the boundaries and exploring the possibilities of that marginal "woman's space."

BUCHI EMECHETA

Buchi Emecheta was born near Lagos in 1944 and has been living in London since 1962. She has written ten novels, including the now classic novel *The*

Joys of Motherhood (1979). In *The Joys of Motherhood* Emecheta shows how the traditional background and experiences of a village woman, Nnu Ego, become dysfunctional in Lagos. Her attack on the "joys" of motherhood in Nigeria is a sophisticated analysis of the betrayal of women in colonial and postcolonial Africa.

Nnu Ego is brought to Lagos before World War II to marry Nnaife, a man she has never met. This is her second marriage. When she meets Nnaife, his potbelly, pale skin and demeaning job (washerman to a white family) are shocking to her. A friend of Nnu Ego's underscores the problem: "Men here are too busy being white men's servants to be men" (Emecheta 51). Gender roles are dependent on appearance and status, as well as sex; without the appearance or the work of a typical male, Nnaife is seen as "a middle-aged woman" (Emecheta 42). These remarks foreshadow Nnu Ego's own struggles to maintain her identity in the antagonistic urban space of Lagos.

At first, they live in one room in the "boys' quarters" belonging to Dr. and Mrs. Meers, Nnaife's employers. The name "boys' quarters" itself is a reminder that this is a space designed for the servants of Europeans, imagined, again, not to be men, but boys. Nnu Ego herself is not supposed to be present at all—these quarters were designed as if servants did not have families. To Nnu Ego, the place is initially disgusting: "This place, this square room painted completely white like a place of sacrifice" (Emecheta 46). In this image, the squareness of the room and its whiteness identify it as a European-designed space, which, reinterpreted in Nnu Ego's aesthetic and architectural categories, is awkward, even ominous: "a place of sacrifice." The Meers' proximity to the boys' quarters controls certain aspects of Nnu Ego's behavior: she is not allowed to make noise, and her pregnancy has to be hidden from Mrs. Meers. When her baby son dies, even her grief has to be restrained. The arrangement of the Meers' compound, with the boys' quarters within the grounds but not actually part of the house, is a classic example of the architecture of colonialism. The architectural environment has political and social relations of power built into it.

Shaheen Haque has asserted in her discussion of British architects' plans for low income housing in England that white male middle-class architects "create the physical environment in which we live and reinforce through their designs their problematic definitions of women, Black people and the working classes" (Haque 34). Similarly, the Meers' compound suits their needs, but forces Nnu Ego to accept a foreign geometry and design for her home. Further, the design of the compound forces her to repress her feelings and make her behavior conform to the Meers' standards, not just in their presence, but even when she is alone within her apartment. The size, location and design of the boys' quarters reinforce the unequal relations of power between the white masters and the black servants.

Nnu Ego's pregnancy is supposed to reconcile her to her new situation; her husband says he has given her everything a woman wants. After the birth, Nnu Ego herself agrees to this, saying "He has made me into a real woman" (Emecheta 53). Her motherhood is central to her sense of self, and makes her content with her husband Nnaife and their life in Lagos. Nnu Ego's baby son dies, however, when he is only four weeks old; Nnu Ego discovers his body lying on the floor mat in their apartment. The loss of her baby, the loss of motherhood, almost drives her insane. She flees through Lagos, gradually determining to drown herself by throwing herself off a bridge. These scenes, which open the novel, show Nnu Ego to be completely disassociated from her environment: "Nnu Ego backed out of the room, her eyes unfocused and glazed, looking into vacancy. Her feet were light and she walked as if in a daze, not conscious of using those feet. She collided with the door" (7). Without her child, she feels no connection to her surroundings, and brushes past buildings and people without seeing them. Her grief is caused by the loss of her baby; Nnu Ego, who was barren in her first marriage, now feels that she will never have a child that lives, never be a mother.

Even in Lagos, the flight of a young woman so clearly in distress arouses people's concern: "She dodged the many who tried to help her" (Emecheta 8). Emecheta shows that there is still a sense of community in Lagos' urban environment. On the bridge itself, a crowd grows as a man tries to prevent Nnu Ego from killing herself. Emecheta reveals both the crowd's idle curiosity and their underlying values:

[The crowd] appreciated this free entertainment, though none of them wanted the woman to achieve her suicidal aim . . . a thing like that is not permitted in Nigeria; you are simply not allowed to commit suicide in peace, because everyone is responsible for the other person. (Emecheta 60)

Here, Emecheta claims that there is a national ethic of behavior in Nigeria, a code that transcends ethnic and regional divisions. In Lagos, that code is present, but somewhat fragile; people are anxious to get to work, and can see Nnu Ego's behavior as entertainment, even as they try to stop her. Providentially, a friend of Nnaife's arrives and recognizes Nnu Ego, and he is able to convince her to return home. Only someone who knows her is able to dissuade her from suicide.

Nnu Ego gradually becomes accustomed to her new environment, and her one room apartment becomes a reflection of her state of mind. As she begins to accept Lagos standards of material wealth, she improves the room with her savings from petty trading: "They now had attractive mats on the floor, they had polished wooden chairs and new patterned curtains" (Emecheta 54). When Nnu Ego is grieving for her son, Emecheta shows how Nnu Ego's friend Ato "reads" her home to discover the extent of her grief: "Nnu Ego led her into their room, which was unswept; the curtains had gone grey from lack of timely washing and the whole atmosphere was disorderly. Ato, knowing how clean and meticulous her friend normally was, tactfully said nothing" (74).

Emecheta emphasizes the interrelationship between women and their immediate environment: their feelings, desires and creativity are written on the walls of the homes that they maintain. Traditionally, West African women decorate their own homes, painting the walls with designs and symbols that are drawn from their culture and are expressive of the individual woman's creativity. These designs continue to be produced today, examples of an African art form that is uniquely female: "Wall and body motifs . . . are a woman's response to the world around her and, above all, adorn her home, enhancing an otherwise cheerless landscape" (Courtney-Clarke 156). Emecheta uses Ato's reading of Nnu Ego's room to show how Nnu Ego's creativity is limited to the choice of furnishings, and to the habit of cleanliness. She is unable, for example, to paint the outside walls of her home, or to add to them; living in the boys' quarters of the Meers' compound, she would not be allowed to express herself so publicly. Ato's readings of Nnu Ego's room are readings of the inadequate space alloted to African women in a Western-designed home.

Nnu Ego learns to adjust to Lagos; her husband gets a different job and they move into a new apartment with their growing family. Traditional practices clash with modern living when Nnaife's older brother dies and Nnaife inherits his four wives, one of whom comes to live in their one room apartment. The added burdens of the new wife, her daughter and the children she has by Nnaife ultimately cause a collapse of the family; so many people can't be fed on Nnaife's salary, or live under one roof. The urban compression of living space makes traditional polygamous relationships unbearable.

Ibuza, Nnu Ego's native village, is described in strong contrast to the impersonal, Westernized architecture and urban anonymity of Lagos. Here, where Nnu Ego was born, the organization of the compound reflects the social ordering within the family: her father's hut is in the middle of the courtyard, surrounded by the huts of his wives. In this world, Nnu Ego has an acknowledged and respected role. Emecheta, while acknowledging that motherhood is the central concern of women in Ibuza society, describes a society that can allow for exceptions. In Nnu Ego's first marriage, she fails to have a child and must return to her father's compound, yet the women there make her feel that she is a welcome member of their extended family. This is the environment in which Nnu Ego is most at ease: "Nnu Ego sat contentedly in front of the hut she had to herself, enjoying the cool of the evening" (Emecheta 156). Here, the larger living spaces within the compound allow for less stressful relationships between family members, and the agricultural economy offers some security: "If it came to the worst, she could always plant her food at the back of her hut" (219). Yet Nnu Ego finds only a temporary respite for herself in Ibuza. Having married Nnaife, whose work is in Lagos, she can only visit, not return to, her native village.

Nnu Ego's daily life is lived most intensely within the home. Lagos, for her, is made up of isolated locations: markets, bridges, and the places where she has lived. She has only a vague idea of the world outside of Lagos and Ibuza; she hears of the end of World War II "when people began saying that the war was over, that the enemy, whoever he was, had killed himself" (Emecheta 171). Nnu Ego's sketchy understanding of international events reflects her vision of the world, firmly centered on her family and her family's interests. The novel itself, however, is located within an international political and economic horizon: the Meers leave for England and Nnaife is sent off to Burma because of World War

II; Nnu Ego's sons leave Nigeria for the United States and Canada in search of better economic opportunities. Lemuel Johnson's remark that "in *The Joys of Motherhood*, Emecheta is running Igbo culture through an enormously complex international geography" (personal communication) seems particularly apt. While Nnu Ego's perspective is limited, the reader can see that her family's history is caught in a web of international concerns.

Within *The Joys of Motherhood*, the significant boundaries are Ibuza, Lagos, and the international horizons of colonialism, World War II, and Western capitalism. National politics are conspicuously absent, in contrast to many African novels by men. Ibuza and Lagos, for example, are usually represented in opposition to each other, rather than as two aspects of a national Nigerian community. This may be the result of the circumstances of the creation of the text: although the novel is set in the time period around World War II, Emecheta wrote it after the Biafran war. The nascent Igbo nation-state was defeated, and forcibly reintegrated into Nigeria. Thus it is not surprising that *The Joys of Motherhood* does not have a strong national boundary. In addition, while the most significant contrast between Ibuza and Lagos is that between the traditional village and a Westernized city, there is also an ethnic difference. Lagos is primarily a Yoruba community, within which the Igbo immigrants are a small minority. Although Emecheta doesn't emphasize ethnic conflict in this novel, part of the characters' sense of isolation and alienation in Lagos comes from their position as part of a minority community.

Nnu Ego's life does have a larger, spiritual horizon, which is an integral part of her experience of the world. Nnu Ego's family believes that she inherited the malevolent spirit of a slave girl, murdered to serve her mistress (a member of Nnu Ego's family) in the afterlife. This spirit is blamed for Nnu Ego's initial inability to conceive a child, and figures in her dreams throughout her life, giving her babies but taunting her at the same time. Nnu Ego herself, after her death, is supplicated as a spirit by her grandchildren. Because she has had eight children, they believe she will help them conceive, yet she "refuses": "However many people appealed to her to make women fertile, she never did" (224). This spiritual horizon expands the novel into the past and the future, and suggests that Nnu Ego, a tormented woman in human life, has freedom and power in the afterlife. The slave woman protests against her inhuman treatment; Nnu Ego protests the virtual enslavement of women in motherhood by refusing children to her descendants. Emecheta is very careful in her description of spiritual beliefs; her narrative neither asserts nor denies the validity of Nnu Ego's spritual powers. The slave girl's spirit may be a real influence on Nnu Ego's life, or a dream figure, created by her family's mythology. Nnu Ego's "refusal" to help her grandchildren conceive may be simply the silence of the grave. Yet the image of the slave girl's spirit shows how Nnu Ego (and her family) sees her life interacting transgenerationally within the family, and the time span of the novel is extended beyond the limits of her own life.

In traditional Igbo societies, Nnu Ego's numerous children would have been her guarantee of an honorable and prosperous old age. Certainly, it would have been expected that her children would house and clothe her.   Yet Nnu Ego is disappointed here as well, caught in the social upheaval created by Western colonization in Nigeria.   Her two eldest male children, educated in British style schools, leave Nigeria for Canada and the United States.   Their dislocation makes them unavailable to their mother, even if they had seen it as their duty to support her; Oshia, her eldest son, refuses his father's direct request for help with the family's expenses. Oshia has accepted Western ideas of individual ambition and self-sufficiency, and will not accept any responsibility for his extended family. Instead of being cared for by her children, Nnu Ego dies by the roadside: "She died quietly there, with no child to hold her hand and no friend to talk to her" (Emecheta 224).   Motherhood, which should have guaranteed and strengthened her connection to the land, has betrayed her; her death is the death of the homeless, the abandoned.

In the course of the novel, Emecheta provides a description of the disjunction between the urban, Westernized environment of colonial Lagos and Ibuza culture: the architecture of Lagos is itself hostile to the preservation of large, polygamous households. In this way, Emecheta emphasizes the interrelationship between society and landscape; the landscape of the village, the compound and the separate huts is created by and suited to a traditional life. Lagos, that amalgam of Western imitations, is hostile to it. The new urban landscape of Africa demands a new kind of society.

While Emecheta critiques contemporary attitudes towards women and the "double bind" of the collision of African and Western culture, she provides only a limited image of the African landscape. The contrast of the Westernized city and the traditional village is a commonplace in African literature, and reinforces the image of traditional societies as static havens from the modern world. Perhaps this is the result of Emecheta's own life history.

Emecheta did not grow up in a village. She describes herself as an observer of rural life: "I was intrigued by the whole way of life. For example, some women will sit for hours just peeling egusi (melon seed) or tying the edge of cloth" (Emecheta interview, in James, *In Their Own Voices* 37). In *The Joys of Motherhood*, while Ibuza life is valued, there are few descriptions of what women's work entailed, other than the care of children; it may be that Emecheta did not feel she knew enough about other experiences in village life to describe them.

Before she became a writer, Emecheta left Nigeria for England, which has been her principal residence since that time (except for a stint at the University of Port Harcourt). In England, she has become critical of African English and African literature: "My vehicle is the English language and staying in this society, working in it, you master the nuances. Writing coming from Nigeria, from Africa (I know this because my son does the criticism) sounds quite stilted" (James 39). She feels that women in Nigeria "are riddled with hypocrisy" (38). For Emecheta, Nigeria has become a foreign country: "I find I don't fit in there anymore" (38). In light of these feelings, it is easier to understand the sweeping criticism of Nigerian society in *The Joys of Motherhood*: no one in Ibuza or in

Lagos is, finally, willing to support Nnu Ego. Her loneliness, and her death by the roadside, may be not only an appeal to Emecheta's audience to address the problems of African women, but also a figuration of the exile, alone in a strange land. The landscape of *The Joys of Motherhood* is a description written from a distance. It combines Emecheta's fond memories of village life with her reasons for leaving Nigeria; it is the landscape of memory and desire. Her most recent novels have focused on the experience of immigrants in Britain. The landscape of Africa, in Emecheta's life and works, has faded into the background.

MARIAMA BÂ

Mariama Bâ writes from within Senegalese culture, specifically Senegalese Islamic culture. In her novel *So Long a Letter*, she explores the space allotted to women, especially the constricted space allotted to widows. The landscape of the novel is extremely restricted; only in imagination and memory does Ramatoulaye leave the confines of her home. By limiting her perspective to Ramatoulaye's, Bâ recreates for her reader the horizons of an African Islamic woman's experience.

So Long a Letter consists of a series of letters written by Ramatoulaye Fall to her friend Aissatou Bâ, while Ramatoulaye is observing the Islamic custom of four months and ten days of mourning for her husband, during which she does not leave her house. It is a withdrawal into herself:

My heart concurs with the demands of religion. Reared since childhood on their strict precepts, I expect not to fail. The walls that limit my horizon for four months and ten days do not bother me. I have enough memories in me to ruminate upon. (Bâ 8)

Five years previously, Ramatoulaye had been faced with a crisis. Her husband, Modou Fall, had taken a second wife, a girl the same age as his eldest daughter. In similar circumstances, Aissatou had divorced her husband, traveled abroad, and become a successful interpreter living in America. Ramatoulaye decides not to divorce Modou and to accept the marriage, but Modou, rather than obeying traditional Islamic precepts and sharing time equally with his wives, abandons Ramatoulaye and moves in with his second wife. After his sudden death by heart attack, Ramatoulaye uses the period of mourning to consider the wisdom of her decisions.

Ramatoulaye is part of a changing society: "It was the privilege of our generation to be the link between two periods in our history, one of domination, the other of independence. . . . With independence achieved, we witnessed the birth of a republic, the birth of an anthem and the implantation of a flag" (Bâ 25). Ramatoulaye, unlike Nnu Ego, is well-educated and aware of national political issues; she sees herself as a participant in a national movement towards modernization. Yet Ramatoulaye's life has been molded by Islamic practices which control women's access to public space.

Her contradictory religious and educational backgrounds create the roots of the conflict. Brought up in a rural village with Aissatou, Ramatoulaye grew up accepting Islam, but she was sent to a Western-style school which emphasized radically different values.

In her descriptions of her home, Ramatoulaye emphasizes discrete images:

heat and dazzlement, the woodfires, the sharp green mango, bitten into in turns, a delicacy in our greedy mouths. I close my eyes. Ebb and tide of images: drops of sweat beading your mother's ochre-coloured face as she emerges from the kitchen, the procession of young wet girls chattering on their way back from the springs. (Bâ 1)

These images evoke the traditional rural village. In her remembrances, her childhood home is a community of women: she recalls mothers, grandmothers, young girls and even "fairy godmothers;" the only males in her description are children. Ramatoulaye's relationship with Aissatou springs from this female community.

Ramatoulaye was then sent to a French high school established to prepare African girls for their role in a modernized, Westernized society:

To lift us out of the bog of tradition, superstition and custom, to make us appreciate a multitude of civilizations without renouncing our own, to raise our vision of the world, cultivate our personalities, strengthen our qualities, to make up for our inadequacies, to develop universal moral values in us: these were the aims of our admirable headmistress. (Bâ 15-16)

Ramatoulaye admires these qualities without hesitation; her life is an exploration of the ways to integrate these Western goals with the expectations of an Islamic African society.

Her image of this school is idealized:

Do you remember the morning train that took us for the first time to Ponty-Ville, the teachers' training college in Sebikotane?

Ponty-Ville is the countryside still green from the last rains, a celebration of youth right in the middle of nature, banjo music in dormitories transformed into dance floors, conversations held along the rows of geraniums or under the thick mango trees. (Bâ 13)

Rains, youth, green countrysides—Ponty-Ville is described as a veritable garden of Eden created for French African youth. The combination of geraniums and mango trees suggests the hybrid ideal of French West Africa. Somewhat defensively, Ramatoulaye asserts that her celebration of this education is not a betrayal of her country: "The path chosen for our training and our blossoming has not been at all fortuitous. It has accorded with the profound choices made by New Africa for the promotion of the black woman" (Bâ 16).

Ramatoulaye's integration of Western and Senegalese values develops throughout the novel. She works as a teacher, yet, with the help of servants and Western gadgets, maintains traditional standards of hospitality in her home:

His [Modou Fall's] mother would stop by again and again while on her outings, always flanked by different friends, just to show off her son's social success but particularly so that they might see, at close quarters, her supremacy in this beautiful house in which she did not live. (Bâ 19)

Ramatoulaye and her husband learn Western dances and buy gramophones and radios, but Ramatoulaye still dresses in traditional clothes. Thus she attempts to interweave ideas from conflicting cultures.

When Modou Fall marries Binetou, a schoolgirl, he justifies it as "the will of God," and calls on the Imam to visit Ramatoulaye, reveal his marriage, and advise her to accept it. The marriage, however, is in no way traditional. Binetou, in exchange for her reluctant agreement to marry, demands a modern villa, an allowance, and an Alfa-Romeo. This second marriage is the product of the lure of youth and of Western popular culture, as Modou Fall foolishly tries to keep up with the latest fashions. His infatuation with Binetou and her milieu leads Modou Fall to abandon even the appearance of respectability, as he no longer lives with or visits his first wife, Ramatoulaye, and their children. She has been abandoned in all but name.

Ramatoulaye submits to her role as senior wife in a polygamous marriage. Even after Modou's desertion, she continues to act circumspectly and correctly, only allowing herself two nontraditional pleasures: driving a car and going to the cinema. The car is a gift from Aissatou, but also a challenge; Ramatoulaye must learn how to drive. It also allows Ramatoulaye to feel less humiliated, as her co-wife Binetou "streaked along the roads in an Alfa Romeo" (Bâ 53). Binetou's car is a bribe, an exchange for her body; Ramatoulaye's Fiat is the reward of friendship and a gift of independence from one woman to another.

The cinema is similarly both a pleasure and a rebellion against the situation in which Modou has left her:

People stared at the middle-aged lady without a partner. I would feign indifference, while anger hammered against my nerves and the tears I held back welled up behind my eyes.
From the surprised looks, I gauged the slender liberty granted to women. (Bâ 51)

These are small rebellions enacted within the context of an Islamic society: unlike Aissatou, Ramatoulaye does not reject her traditional roles. On the contrary, she honors the roles assigned to women:

Those women we call "house"-wives deserve praise. The domestic work they carry out, and which is not paid in hard cash, is essential to the home. (63) One is a mother in order to understand the inexplicable. One is a mother to lighten the darkness . . . one is a mother in order to love without beginning or end. (Bâ 82-83)

Within her own home, Ramatoulaye is the centerpiece; sitting on a mat "reserved for [her] use only" (Bâ 79), she receives visitors, dispenses advice, and cares for her children. She sees the household as an organic being, and herself as its heart: "My heart beats monotonously under my black wrappers. How I like to listen to this slow rhythm! A new substance is trying to graft itself on to the household" (86). The "new substance" is her daughter's lover; through her children, Ramatoulaye continues to be exposed to the changing values of her society. Catching her daughters smoking, she wonders: "Does it mean one can't have modernism without a lowering of moral standards?" (77). And yet, when her daughter Aissatou confesses that she is pregnant with her lover's child, Ramatoulaye's reaction is based on her motherhood, and not on her religion:

At this moment of confrontation, I realized how close I was to my child. The umbilical cord took on new life, the indestructible bond beneath the avalanche of storms and the duration of time. . . . Her life and her future were at stake, and these were powerful considerations, overriding all taboos and assuming greater importance in my heart and in my mind. (Bâ 83)

Motherhood, the connection between mother and daughter, here becomes a ground for rebelling against traditional Islamic law. Ramatoulaye, rather than casting off her daughter, forgives and supports her, meeting her lover and agreeing to their marriage. Her friend, Farmata, the marriage broker, is astonished at her behavior: "To give a sinner so much attention was beyond her" (Bâ 84). Ramatoulaye's motherhood connects her to the future, to modern Senegal, rather than acting as a conservative cultural bond, as Oladele Taiwo has theorized, motherhood "helps to maintain the continuity of the ethnic group and the race" (Taiwo 2). The emotional bond of motherhood gives Ramatoulaye the courage to defy authority, even though she had been unwilling to do so on her own behalf.

Ramatoulaye, by the end of *So Long a Letter*, has not only surveyed the constricted space allotted to women, but has also begun to move into the public space of the city, in defiance of cultural expectations. She drives her own car, goes to the cinema, and engages in political discussions: "I widen my scope by taking an interest in current world affairs" (Bâ 88). According to Iris Marion Young, women's relationship to space is mediated (and inhibited) by cultural expectations about women. As our bodies move through space, we orient ourselves to our environment: "There is a world for a subject just insofar as the body has capacities by which it can approach, g[r]asp, and appropriate its surroundings in the direction of its intentions" (Young 58). In her essay, "Throwing Like a Girl: A Phenomenology of Feminine Body Comportment, Motility and Spatiality," Young posits a feminine experience of space as having a dual structure. Women confine their movements to a limited space surrounding themselves; the space beyond this constricted area is not perceived as available to their movement (hence "throwing like a girl," when a girl keeps her elbows in and moves only within a restricted space). The space beyond is visually but not physically available: "The space of the 'yonder' exists for feminine existence, but only as that which she is looking into rather than moving in" (Young 63). While Young's theory is based on white American women's experience, the dual structure of space is also relevant here; Ramatoulaye, having fulfilled the role of wife and mother, is now exploring the "yonder," the public space of the nation.

Mildred Mortimer, in *Journeys Through the French African Novel*, emphasizes the importance of Islamic religious law in structuring the novel. Mortimer sees Islam as structuring not only Ramatoulaye's enclosure but her disclosure, her letters to Aissatou: "*Mirasse*, an Islamic precept, calls for the disclosure of all possessions of the deceased for the purpose of inheritance. . . . Ramatoulaye broadens the definition of disclosure to unveil Modou's emotional breach of faith in their marriage" (138-39). Mortimer interprets Ramatoulaye's journey into her self as a move compensating for women's lack of opportunity for outward journeys:

In other words, unable to embark upon the journey that results in knowledge gained through enriching experience, Ramatoulaye turns to the inner journey that provides knowledge through self-examination and maturity through personal transformation. (Mortimer 137)

At the end of this journey (but still within the Islamic enclosure), Ramatoulaye finds the courage to reject new suitors: she has paid her debt to Islam, and need not take on another husband. Her previous acceptance of Modou's second marriage now gives her power. She obeyed the Imam, she remained faithful to Modou, she is respecting the laws for mourning—so she is free now to choose a life for herself. The nervousness of the men in her community respecting her freedom can be seen in the urgency and frequency of her suitors. Ramatoulaye herself is aware of her potential for a new, more powerful role: "I can feel new buds springing up in me" (Bâ 89). Thus Ramatoulaye has created a role for herself, both within the home and within her community, that integrates her need for independence with her respect for Islamic traditions. While she admires Aissatou's choice of a completely Westernized lifestyle, Ramatoulaye is confident about her own choice, to the point of being able to tease Aissatou about her Western ways:

Used to living far away, you will want—again, I have taken a bet with Daba—table, plate, chair, fork.
    More convenient, you will say. But I will not let you have your way. I will spread out a mat. On it there will be the big, steaming bowl into which you will have to accept that other hands dip. (Bâ 89)

I have included *So Long a Letter* (even though it is written in French) in this study because it is a classic African novel. It reveals how women's prescribed enclosure and self-examination can lead to liberation and power. Bâ's heroine seeks a solution to her dual education. Her journey, however, takes place only within herself. Thus the landscape of the novel is limited to a small number of locations. The most important horizon is circumscribed by the walls of her home—the space which Ramatoulaye has created for herself and her family, and within which she accomplishes her transformation. Ramatoulaye's creation of this space, which is both supremely her own and firmly within the Islamic context, allows her the freedom to negotiate the "yonder"—to venture out into public space. The prayer mat and the Fiat represent Ramatoulaye's integration of Islam and Western individualism.

ZAYNAB ALKALI

Zaynab Alkali is from Borno State, Nigeria, and her first novel is set in an Islamic community in Northern Nigeria. In Alkali's novel *The Stillborn*, in contrast to *So Long a Letter*, the experience of enclosure is not liberating but suffocating; education and experience in the outside world are necessary for her heroine to take control of her life within the enclosure.

Alkali's heroine, Li, feels that life inside her father's compound is "worse than a prison" (Alkali 3). She is "trapped and unhappy" (3). The organization of the compound, with her father's hut in the middle where "he could see everything that went on in his compound" (8) reifies the social and moral constraints on a young Muslim girl in Northern Nigeria.

The grandfather, Kaka, who also lives in the compound, is sympathetic to his grandchildren, and concerned about the restrictions placed on them: "Children shouldn't be caged, he reasoned, for if the cage got broken by accident or design, they would find the world too big to live in" (Alkali 25). This proverb is borne out by the plot of the novel: all the children are unprepared for the challenges of life outside the enclosure. Significantly, Li sneaks out one night for a dance by making a hole in the fence around the compound, escaping like a prisoner. Her father, Baba, when he discovers the hole, acts like a warder:

He stood, feet apart and arms akimbo, scowling at a large opening in the fence behind mama's hut. When he saw that they had all assembled, he turned to face them.

"Who went out last night?" he asked, looking at them one by one in his usual direct way. (20)

Baba's grilling of the assembled children shows his anger at any infringement of his authority, and especially at any erosion of his control of the space of the compound—nothing should happen within this space that he does not approve beforehand.

The compound is set in a village in Northern Nigeria:

The smaller side of the village was less crowded. It consisted of farmland and a few scattered mud huts which appeared quiet and deserted.

On the opposite and larger side, however, flourished a long stretch of fruit trees, richly dressed in green. Further down, the village lay sprawled in clusters of thatched mud huts. The sun's reflection on the few zinc roofs that were scattered among the clusters threw a blinding light across the village. (Alkali 2)

The village is divided into two classes by a river that separates them. The larger, wealthier side of the village is mixed; not all of the houses have thatched roofs. The "few zinc roofs" show the beginning influence of Western ideas of design in the village; their "blinding light" is an ominous sign of the changes they foreshadow in the architecture and social structure of the village community. Already separations are being made, distinctions are being drawn.

These distinctions are even more obvious in the differences between the European and African parts of the village:

At the base of the hills was the European quarters known as the Hill Station. The houses here were built of stones and roofed with asbestos. Built on a much higher plane and facing the rest of the village, they had assumed the look of an overlord. This advantageous position was further heightened by a thick overgrowth of trees that shrouded the houses, giving them the desired privacy. (Alkali 2)

The building materials, location, and design of these houses all reinforce the superior social status of the Europeans, who work at the mission school and the hospital. The desire for privacy, especially, emphasizes the Europeans' desire to distance themselves from the rest of the population. A further status symbol in the European community is electricity: the Hill Station has its own generator. While the Nigerians have no access to its electricity, the sound of the generator regulates their lives:

At exactly ten o'clock, the sound of the generator that had kept up a regular beating to the rhythm of the heartbeat of every child born for that generation, would die down, signalling the hour of sleep and releasing the night to the walking witches and discontented spirits. (Alkali 2)

While the Europeans maintain their own privacy, their generator invades the privacy of everyone else in the village. Alkali's narrator associates the limits of electrical power with the religious power of the missionaries; when their lights are not on, their religion is no longer in control.

In the compound, Li dreams of life in the city: "The image of a big European house full of houseboys and maids rose before her. Li smiled to herself. The bushy stream, the thorny hillside and the dusty market would soon be forgotten, in the past" (Alkali 55). Li marries Habu, thinking, "The future was in their hands. The world was full of wonderful and exciting things. And were they not young and eager and ready to enjoy life to the fullest?" (57). Li eventually joins Habu in the (unnamed) city, only to be disillusioned.

The city is damaging not as a place, but as an idea: the dreams of easy money and easy living corrupt Habu and his friends. Instead of becoming a doctor, Habu has become a salesman; he has also taken another wife in the city, without telling Li. When Li comes to join him in the city, Habu "stared at Li unflinchingly as if he had never seen her before, then he turned to his brother and complained loudly about the 'cast offs' from the village. He didn't have enough room to house such 'useless articles'" (Alkali 69). These articles are Li's bridewealth: stools, mats, calabashes, and clay pots. All of these would be essential in setting up a new home in the village, but are nearly useless in the city, especially since Habu's tastes have been influenced by Western standards of living. Both Li and Habu are bitterly disappointed, having had fantasies of life in the city that were based on European, and not African standards; Habu will never make enough money to be able to afford the luxurious house and servants that Li had wanted.

Li, warned by a dream, returns to her village when her father dies:

> She found her ancestral home deserted and all the huts in a state of ruin. Some of the walls were crumbling, others had their roofs and doors caved in. Bushes had grown around the compound and it was almost impassable. . . . Although the huts were in ruin, all were still standing except for her father's. She moved to the spot where her father's hut had once been and saw a heap of red soil. (Alkali 74)

In this dream, the father's death results in the physical collapse of the compound—his will held it together. The bushes and wild animals which he had held at bay now press around the remaining buildings. Her father's hut, a symbol of his authority, is not merely in ruin, but erased; in the dream, this terrifies her and she gives a "heart-rending wail" (Alkali 74).

When Li returns home, she finds the compound a shambles. Without her father's protection, the rest of the family seems unable to take care of itself. Once again, she feels a prisoner at home, and vows "to go back into the world and make an independent life for herself" (Alkali 85). After attending a teacher's college she will "assume the role of the 'man of the house' in her father's compound" (85).

In this way, Li not only breaks out of her prison, but transforms it: eventually she builds "a huge modern and enviable building" (Alkali 101) in the compound. She is now the man of the house, replacing her father, and she creates a new architecture which eliminates the controlling central hut of her father's time. The enclosure is now her own. Like Ramatoulaye, Li gains her position through economic independence based on education. Also like Ramatoulaye, Li, while flirting with the idea of liaisons during her long stay in the village, remains faithful to her estranged husband.

After Li's renovations, the compound is no longer arranged in its traditional structure. Li's village is also no longer the traditional village. More generators, kerosene lamps, zinc roofs, more people: "Awa was right after all, when she had said, 'We needn't go to the city, the city will come to us'" (Alkali 94). Where Bâ's novel celebrates the integration of the traditional and the modern, of Western and Islamic practices in Ramatoulaye's creation of her home, Alkali's novel records the dismantling of traditional architectural and social structures. Li's return to her husband and the city reveals that she has come to terms with the past, and is now ready to move beyond it.

Li has a daughter, Shuwa, born at the time of Li's father's death. When Li leaves to go to a teacher's college, she leaves Shuwa behind, in the care of Li's older sister, Awa. At first, Shuwa seems relatively unimportant to Li—she is only one of the many family members Li hopes to support with her teaching salary. When Li sees Shuwa in her sister's home, she is happy at first that the child doesn't ask about her father (Habu), or seem any different from her cousins. Shuwa's birth, however, has given Li a positive connection to the village compound, replacing her ambivalent relationship to her father, and it confirms her desire to improve and rebuild the compound.

In the novel, Alkali also makes several references to children, and to dreams, that are stillborn or aborted. Habu's other wife aborted their child, and almost lost her life. Faku, Li's friend, is barren, and suffering the humiliation of seeing her co-wife bear children for their husband. She sends a message back to her mother in the village through Li, saying "The land is still brown and unyielding. Not until it is covered with green will I come to the village" (Alkali 80). Li herself had dreamed of her friend tilling a dry and unyielding land. Near the end of the novel, Li dreams again, this time of the future, and imagines herself speaking to her great-granddaughter: "It is also important to remember that like babies dreams are conceived but not all dreams are born alive. Some are aborted. Others are stillborn" (104). This dream leads Li to resolve to return to her husband:

She knew now that the bond that had tied her to the father of her child was not ruptured. And in spite of everything, in the soft cradle of her heart, there was another baby forming. This time Li was determined the baby would not be stillborn. (Alkali 104-105)

Children and dreams are inextricably intertwined in Li's thinking. Her dream of the future reassures her that her child Shuwa will live, and will have children of her own; the dream in turn makes her accept her child as a connection to her estranged husband. The new baby in "the soft cradle of her heart" is a dream of reconciliation.

These passages enrich the meaning of the title of the novel: Li's child isn't stillborn, but her dream of city life is. By the time she reaches the city, Habu has already taken another wife, and any chance they had of reaching their ideal standard of living in the city is lost. Li painfully reaches that dream alone by educating herself, and raising a European-style building within the old compound of her family. Yet, when she fulfills her goal, Li "felt empty" (Alkali 102). The dream is stillborn. Her new dream of reconciliation will, she hopes, bring a new relationship to her husband: "side by side we will learn to walk" (105). Out of this reconciliation, there is also the possibility of more children, and more dreams.

At the end of the novel, Li determines to return to the city, and to Habu, bringing Shuwa with her. Alkali's novel is unusual in its repetition of the move from village to city; Li, in effect, moves out of her home three times. In each move, however, Li has made a new adjustment. In the first move to the city, Li's dreams of a European house with maids and houseboys is destroyed, along with her illusions about her husband. In her first return, Li acknowledges her familial responsibilities, but must once again leave in order to fulfill them. Her second journey is one of education and economic independence. In her second return, Li fulfills her familial responsibilities, becoming the father of the household and restructuring the compound. Li is able to renovate the private space of the compound after her experience of more public spaces. And yet Li is, at the end of the novel, once more determined to leave for the city. This ending suggests that while Li has transformative power within the village, it is now too small, too confined a space for her abilities. Educated, independent, and secure in her motherhood, Li now plans to create a more equal relationship with her husband, and perhaps change life in the city as she has changed it in the compound. Alkali leaves her heroine moving onto a wider canvas, with her daughter beside her.

In each of the three novels I have discussed, the authors explore the space of motherhood, and describe the restrictions and limitations of that space. In Emecheta's novel, however, the protagonist, Nnu Ego, is unable to move outside of that space, and dies lamenting the crumbling of traditional roles. In both Bâ's and Alkali's novels, we see women who are determined to move outward, away from the village, away from the enclosure. Yet in both works, the women make these moves only after fulfilling traditional expectations: marrying, bearing children. Ramatoulaye still centers her life within the household. For some, these novels may represent too slow, too gradual a process for changing women's status in African Islamic societies. Yet Alkali and Bâ expand the horizons of women's space, testing the limits, moving outwards.

By writing novels, African women challenge the established male tradition. In addition to Bâ and Emecheta, Flora Nwapa and Ama Ata Aidoo have claimed a space in African literature for women, a space which is being explored, reconfigured and expanded by a younger generation of writers, including Zaynab Alkali. This fictional space is as much a part of the geography of their novels as the countries in which they set their fiction.

These novels also challenge the nationalist discourses that occur both within and outside of literature: "Where women tell of their own experience, they map their own geography, scry their own history and so, necessarily, contest official representations of a nationalist reality" (Boehmer 10-11). Thus *So Long a Letter*, while representing Mariama Bâ's enthusiasm for national independence, also reveals the limits of that independence for women. *The Joys of Motherhood* inscribes the intersections of Igbo culture and international imperial discourses, with only minimal attention to the national discourse of Nigeria. In Alkali's novel, even the city is left unnamed; the city is more important in the novel as an ideal instilled in Li and Habu as adolescents than as a specific geopolitical space. The nation gets even less attention. Rather, Alkali's heroine feels the effects first of parental authority, and then of religious and social codes that restrict women's behavior. The descriptions of women's space in these novels implicitly question the significance of the horizon of the nation for women's lives.

African women's writing is African literature with a difference; it is women's writing with a difference. Common threads mingle in their works: motherhood, womanhood, identity, education, Westernization, tradition; but each writer weaves them together in her own way, creating different patterns. Reading their works as a dialogue, we can begin to see a complex geography of overlapping territories and uncertain boundaries: the space of African women's literature.

NOTE

1. In *Devil on the Cross*, however, Ngugi provides a figure of a modern woman who is not a prostitute, but an auto mechanic: Jacinta Wariinga. Her character shows Ngugi rethinking women's roles from a Marxist perspective, emphasizing the importance of labor, not just for economic security, but for establishing the foundation for Wariinga's social relationships and identification with the country.

Chapter 3

The Landscape of Religion in West African Literature by Men

Even before Ngugi wa Thiong'o published his first novel, the image of Africa was being reshaped by African writers. Writing in response to Western texts of exploration and colonization, authors such as Chinua Achebe sought to contest the European-centered image of Africa. This challenge was made doubly difficult by the position of the African author: often Western-educated, often writing for a Western press and a Western audience, his own environment was permeated with Western ideas and influences. The desire of Chinweizu and others "to end all foreign domination of African culture, to systematically destroy all encrustations of colonial and slave mentality, to clear the bushes and stake out new foundations for a liberated African modernity" (Chinweizu 1) was a desire to root out Western elements of their own education and environment.

The representation of religious beliefs in the landscape intersects with the issue of Westernization in a variety of ways. Indigenous African religions provide African writers with visions of Africa which run counter to the Western, colonizing tradition, as in Amos Tutuola's *The Palm-Wine Drinkard*. In West Africa, Islam was so well-established as to seem to be part of indigenous culture, although several aspects of pre-Islamic civilizations remained. Cheikh Hamidou Kane explores the intersection of traditional authority, Islam, colonialism, and Christianity in *Ambiguous Adventure*. Christianity of course came into West Africa as part of the Westernization and colonization of Africa, and many African writers expose the suffering Christianity inflicted on Africans as missionaries insisted on the dismantling of indigenous culture. Chinua Achebe's *Things Fall Apart* is the classic novel of the disintegration of a family and a community under the pressure of colonialism and Christianity. Yet Achebe also explores *why* Christianity was able to gain a foothold in African societies. In *Aké: The Years of Childhood* Soyinka depicts a Christianity which has already begun to be integrated with indigenous cultural practices and spiritual beliefs. In each of these texts, the landscape presented by the novel is shaped by the influence of religious beliefs and Westernization.

AMOS TUTUOLA

The first well-known novel from Africa was Amos Tutuola's *The Palm-Wine Drinkard and His Dead Palm-Wine Tapster in the Dead's Town*, published in 1952. Tutuola is a Nigerian writer; his story is a retelling of Yoruba myths and folktales. While his book was enthusiastically received by Western critics, it was often criticized by Africans. The main elements of the controversy were the language of the novel and its use of traditional folktales.[1]

Tutuola's style relies heavily on neologisms and non-English speech patterns:

We slept in that bush, but when it was about two o'clock in the night, there we saw a creature, either he was a spirit or other harmful creature, we could not say, he was coming towards us, he was white as if painted with white paint, he was white from foot to the topmost of his body, but he had no head or feet and hands like human-beings and he got one large eye on his topmost. (Tutuola 41-42)

Dylan Thomas called the language of this story "young English" (Thomas 7), and the work was extremely popular in Europe. European praise for the novel caused a reaction among many African critics, who were disturbed by the image of Africa implied by the ungrammatical use of English and by the retelling of African folktales combined with modern details. As Es'kia Mphahlele has said, "You begin, as he does, by telling a story that has been told a thousand times, and then you simply change the sequence of events and write them in bad English . . . and you have Tutuola" ("Entretien avec Ezekiel Mphahlele" 57). Another South African writer and critic, Peter Abrahams, said "True, we have already had Mr. Tutuola and his *Drinkard* wandering in the twilight world of the *Bush of Ghosts* among tribal monsters where we encounter telephone-voices but never enter the telephone world of the present. The word [sic] of the *Drinkard* is, to my mind, likely to appeal more to non-Africans than to Africans. . . . Mr. Tutuola's *Drinkard* is as incapable of genuine development as is tribalism in the technological present" (Abrahams 975). *The Palm-Wine Drinkard* held the attraction for a Western audience of a completely alien and "primitive" environment, a world of ghosts and strange supernatural creatures. The concern of the African critics was that it would reinforce the Westerners' impression of the African as immersed in a mythical world of the past, unable to come to terms with technology or modern Western society.

The Palm-Wine Drinkard is strongly influenced by the oral tradition. Tutuola uses long, loosely-connected sentences and repetition of phrases and syntactical patterns. In the example above, Tutuola's syntax conveys the excitement and fear of the narrator: "He was coming towards us, he was white from foot to the topmost of his body" (Tutuola 42). In oral performances, there is little need for a lengthy description of fields, villages, and the bush when both the speaker and the audience have a shared understanding of what these look like, and such a description would interfere with the pacing of the story. Tutuola's narrative rarely gives detailed descriptions of the setting; rather, he focuses on the strange, the supernatural, and the unknown (the Dead's Town).

The narrative uses a traditional Yoruba worldview as its physical, social, and cosmological setting. In this world, humans interact freely with spirits and the dead. As Michael Thelwell claims about the *The Palm-Wine Drinkard,* "Out of the interplay of deities, ancestors, and humanity, through a process of mutual obligation expressed in language, ritual, and protocol as handed down by tradition, society became possible. A universe of history, stability, morality, and order was achieved" (Thelwell xvii). Thus the landscape of the novel includes not only the immediate physical world, but also the world of the dead. Spirits can pass freely between the two worlds, and even the Drinkard himself visits the Deads' Town.

The human community creates an ordered world out of chaos, through the buildings, courtyards, streets, marketplaces, and farming plots of the village. This space, however, is surrounded by the bush, which, as Thelwell claims, is disordered and uncontrollable: "Here was the home of chaos, where random spirits without name or history, of bizarre forms and malignant intent were to be found." The storyteller "had free range of this random and arbitrary world" (Thelwell xvii). Tutuola's story is primarily a story of the bush, of the evil and supernatural creatures that the Palm-Wine Drinkard and his wife encounter on their journeys.

The narrator, the Drinkard, emphasizes the dangers of the bush:

In those days, there were many wild animals and every place was covered by thick bushes and forests; again, towns and villages were not near each other as nowadays, and as I was travelling from bushes to bushes and from forests to forests and sleeping inside it for many days and months, I was sleeping on the branches of trees, because spirits, etc. were just like partners, and to save my life from them; and again I could spend two or three months before reaching a town or a village. (Tutuola 9)

There is very little description of the physical characteristics of the bush, except for the unusual places along the journey: "We saw a big tree which was about one thousand and fifty feet in length and about two hundred feet in diameter. This tree was almost white as if it was painted every day with white paint with all its leaves and also branches" (Tutuola 65). This passage is typical; when the narrator describes a supernatural being or environment, he becomes very specific about its size, weight and color, providing his audience with an accurate image of what it was that he encountered. In most references to the bush, however, there is little description; as in the former passage, it is assumed that the audience knows what the bush is like.

The town is the known world, identified not only by its physical characteristics but also by its social relations; an abandoned town is immediately reabsorbed into the bush: "There we met many houses which had been ruined for hundreds of years . . . there we saw an image which sat down on a flat stone, it had two long breasts with deep eyes, it was very ugly and terrible to see" (Tutuola 55-56). As soon as the people are gone, the houses become the homes of supernatural creatures. The world consists of small cleared areas, in which human activities are possible and society thrives, surrounded by and continually threatened by a chaotic, unknown, and malignant forest, in which survival is uncertain at best.

Michael Thelwell suggests that the insecurity of this world may be a reflection of the cultural trauma and alienation of colonialism: the "bush" may represent the overpowering presence of Western civilization, threatening to absorb or destroy Yoruba culture. There are a few modern details in the story; for example, one of the creatures is said to have "a lower voice like a telephone" (Tutuola 35). It seems more accurate, however, to see these as the natural embellishments a storyteller gives the tale as he or she retells it. An oral narrative has elements, sequences, and, often, proverbs or songs which need to be retained if the story is to remain "the same," but within those limits a storyteller can use new images and details to make the story more vivid for his or her audience. Tutuola uses modern images and references that will be familiar to his audience. The fundamental conflict in the story is not between Western civilization and Yoruba culture, but between the human world, including its physical spaces, social organization, and benevolent spirits, and the chaotic world of the bush.

Gerald Moore has said that "Tutuola's books are far more like a fascinating cul-de-sac than the beginning of anything directly useful to other writers" (Moore 57). In the ensuing tradition of West African literature, however, texts by Soyinka, Armah, Awoonor, and Ben Okri have been published that bear similarities in technique, imagery, language, or cosmology to Tutuola's work. Some of these similarities may be based on a shared interest in Yoruba cosmology rather than a direct borrowing from Tutuola. Tutuola's works, however, provide an important link between traditional, pre-independence oral narratives and contemporary fiction; they are reminders of the continuing importance of oral, often pidgin or krio, traditions in contemporary society and in popular market literature during a period when the Queen's English became a requirement for serious literature in Africa.

CHINUA ACHEBE

Things Fall Apart is the classic African novel. It was published in 1958, and was considered "the first English novel in which the life and institutions of a West African people is presented from the inside" (Obumselu 37). The novel is set in the past, just before the arrival of the British in Nigeria, and describes the life of the Igbo people through the story of one man, Okonkwo. Achebe wrote the novel in English, but included Igbo proverbs and syntax to harmonize the dialogue and description with the setting of the novel. This decision was received with enthusiasm by most critics, so much so that Achebe's technique was used as a standard: "[if] there is a faithful reproduction of the speech habits of one people into another language as Mr. Chinua Achebe does significantly in English with the Ibo dialogue proceeding by technique of the proverb, then I think the artist has achieved a reasonable measure of success" (Clark, "Aspects of Nigerian Drama" 125). In *Things Fall Apart*, Achebe proved to a Western critical audience, accustomed to comparing any text in English with canonical British writers, that an African novelist could write a novel in "the Queen's English," and develop plot, characters, dialogue, and setting with as much skill as any British novelist. Achebe also presented that audience with a vision of Africa they had never seen—an African, Igbo-centered, village-centered vision, not travellers' versions of the jungles of the Dark Continent. By including Igbo proverbs and syntactical patterns in his text, Achebe accorded them the same status as Latin tags in the early British novel: a knowledgeable audience would be able to appreciate the subtleties and resonances of the proverbs. In this way, Achebe showed his African audience that their world, their everyday experiences, stories, proverbs, and cosmologies were valid subjects for modern literature, and did not have to be "edited out" to suit the prejudices of a Western audience.

In *Things Fall Apart*, Achebe provides the reader with careful descriptions of the setting. His description provides a complete plan of Okonkwo's compound, allowing the reader to visualize the events which take place there. It is a description directed to a reader unfamiliar with Okonkwo's culture; it helps the Western reader picture the compound, and the unfamiliar elements—Okonkwo's hut, the medicine house—are carefully described and defined. Elements of the novel such as these suggest that at least part of Achebe's intended audience is Western; the novel is designed to show an African perspective on the arrival of the colonists in Nigeria to a Western audience.

The arrangement of Okonkwo's compound implies certain things about the relationships between the people who live there. Okonkwo is a very traditional man; he is concerned about doing things the way they ought to be done. The conventional arrangement of his compound reinforces the reader's sense that Okonkwo wishes to preserve traditional relations between people. For example, the position of the wives' huts, "which together formed a half moon behind the *obi*" (Achebe 10) suggests their subjection to Okonkwo, while the position of his own hut in front of the only opening in the wall around the compound suggests his desire to control the movement of people in and out of his compound. The presence of the "medicine house" is a reminder of Okonkwo's respect for ancestor worship; while he violates other religious laws in his community, he is scrupulous about this one task. His religious belief prepares the reader to understand Okonkwo's horror at his son's conversion to Christianity; without a link to the living, dead spirits are truly dead. The emphasis on the wives, goats, hens, and yams in this description suggests Okonkwo's obsession with prosperity and social status. Prosperity is particularly significant for "age was respected among his people, but achievement was revered" (6). The display of his material wealth within his compound signifies Okonkwo's social status as well as his ability to support and feed his family.

Achebe uses very few descriptive adjectives. He mentions the size, color, and material of objects, but has nothing comparable to, for example, Isak Dinesen's lyrical hyperboles in *Out Of Africa*: "The cicadas sing an endless song in the long grass, smells run along the earth and falling stars run over the sky, like tears over a cheek" (Dinesen 72). The impact of Achebe's description is not meant to be a romantic, sensual experience of the external, material world of the compound; instead, we are encouraged to read through these details the continuing life that is carried on in these surroundings. This is what Leopold Senghor meant by African surrealism:

What moves the Black is not the exterior aspect of the object, it is the *reality*, or better—since "realism" has become sensualism—its *surreality*. Water moves him, not because it cleanses, but because it purifies; fire, because of its destructive powers, not because of its warmth or color. . . . Because here the surface, being understood in its singular particularities, is only the sign of the essence of the object. "The Creator says: Here is the sign." This means that the Negro is a mystic. (Senghor 166)

By focusing the reader's attention on the spatial arrangement of the compound rather than on its visual or sensual impact, Achebe is inviting us to see the compound, not at a particular moment in time, but as the result of the combined effects of the movements of people's lives, particularly the traditional pattern of Okonkwo's life.

Achebe also shows the links between the land and the world of the spirits in *Things Fall Apart*. In the novel, the traditional African worldview divides up the land into compounds, communal spaces, cleared cropland, and the bush. The beneficial gods are associated with the cleared lands and the harvest. The bush, on the other hand, is associated with evil: those whose sickness "was an abomination to the earth" (Achebe 13) are dragged into the forest and left there to die. Ekwefi, Okonkwo's wife, secretly follows a priestess, Chielo, carrying Ekwefi's only child through the forest in the middle of the night. Ekwefi is uncertain about the priestess' purpose, and is afraid that if she is discovered following behind, either she or her child will be harmed. For Ekwefi, the forest at night is not just a physical reality, but an overpowering spiritual presence: "Now she found the half-light of the incipient moon more terrifying than darkness. The world was now peopled with vague, fantastic figures that dissolved under her steady gaze and then formed again in new shapes" (74-75). Chielo's power is associated with the power of these supernatural figures, and thus Ekwefi's fear of being discovered becomes a more generalized fear of being alone, surrounded by supernatural beings:

At one stage Ekwefi was so afraid that she nearly called out to Chielo for companionship and human sympathy. What she had seen was the shape of a man climbing a palm tree, his head pointing to the earth and his legs skywards. But at that very moment Chielo's voice rose again in her possessed chanting, and Ekwefi recoiled, because there was no humanity there. It was not the same Chielo who sat with her in the market. . . . It was a different woman—the priestess of Agbala, the Oracle of the Hills and Caves. (Achebe 75)

The spiritual reality, the figures Ekwefi sees, are more significant to her than the physical details of the forest.

Achebe also describes the effect of changes in weather: "And now the rains had really come, so heavy and persistent that even the village rain-maker no longer claimed to be able to intervene. . . . Sometimes it poured down in such thick sheets of water that earth and sky seemed merged in one grey wetness"(Achebe 24). This description suggests a vision of landscape which is not objective and rational: when the seasons change, it is as if the earth and sky change fundamentally, become one being. The passage comes close to the boundaries of the conventionally narratible: if the earth and sky are one being, there is nothing to differentiate, nothing to describe. Further, if the fusion of earth and sky or the influence of the village rain-maker on the weather were presented as actually existing, the novel would move into a realm of super-natural, mystical experiences. While Tutuola presents supernatural experiences as part of African reality, Achebe keeps the narrative voice firmly within an objective perspective: the narrator reports that the rain-maker's "claims" have changed, whether his powers were ever effective or not, and the world only "seems" to be merged into one grey wetness.

Achebe's narrative control is in the tradition of the English novel: alternative perspectives are entertained, but are implicitly rejected by the narrative voice. Thus radically disruptive ideas can be contained and dismissed or at least set aside, increasing the authority of the narrative voice. And yet, by including these alternative perspectives, Achebe's narrative suggests that another view of these events is possible, a different landscape in which the power of the village rain-maker is real, spirits stalk the forests, and ancestors protect the crops. The title's reference to Yeats's poem suggests that "the center cannot hold;" is this the center of traditional authority, or the "center" of the narrative itself— the objective, rational voice which cannot admit but is also unable to exclude the reality of the supernatural aspects of African life?

When the missionaries come to Mbanta, asking for a piece of land on which to build their church, the elders give them land in the forest: "They did not really want them in their clan, and so they made them that offer which nobody in his right senses would accept" (Achebe 105). When one of the elders says, however, "They boast about victory over death. Let us give them a real battlefield in which to show their victory" (105), Achebe is foreshadowing the Christian interpretation of the location. By building on a piece of land supposedly inhabited by evil spirits, the missionaries are able to show the superiority of their religion simply by staying alive. One of the tragic limitations of the elders of the clan is their inability to grasp the opportunity that this location offers to the Christians.

The conflict between the traditional religion and Christianity becomes, through Okonkwo's killing of a messenger, a conflict between the villagers and the authorities. In this situation, the villagers desert Okonkwo, and in despair, he kills himself, an action unsanctioned by either Christianity or the traditional religion of the village. His suicide is a negation of both systems, the act of a man who could not successfully function in a world where these conflicting horizons are both present.

The rupture his suicide creates is soon smoothed over; the villagers plan to "make sacrifices to cleanse the desecrated land," (Achebe 147) while the Commissioner resolves to mention the incident in his book: "Perhaps not a whole chapter but a reasonable paragraph, at any rate. There was so much else to include, and one must be firm in cutting out details" (148). Because of the power of the colonizers, the Commissioner literally has the last word: the novel ends with the title of the history he plans to write, *The Pacification of the Primitive Tribes of the Lower Niger*.

Achebe's novel moves away from the Western conventional description of landscape by recognizing that competing belief systems will view the same piece of land differently. In addition, the novel shows that, for some, the loss of a certain vision of the world makes it impossible to go on living. Yet the novel has strong links to the Western tradition: the narrator never shares the perspective of the characters, preserving the boundary between the way they see the world and the "reality" of the narrator's objective vision. By the end of the novel, the narrative, the "middle ground" of the novel, the reasonable, objective view which mediates between the misreadings of both the Africans and the colonists, disappears, leaving the two radically conflicting systems inhabiting the same space. Like Okonkwo, it is unable to describe and inhabit a landscape which includes both the traditional and colonial worldviews. The novel ends with the impending inevitable conflict between the colonizer and the colonized; the "space" of the novel, in which the two sides could be controlled and subordinated, has disappeared.

WOLE SOYINKA

In contrast to *Things Fall Apart*, Wole Soyinka's autobiography, *Aké: The Years of Childhood*, intertwines Christian and traditional African imagery, emphasizing the unifying power and comprehensiveness of a child's vision of the world. Soyinka's opening paragraphs highlight those objects that would interest a child:

The sprawling, undulating terrain is all of Aké. More than mere loyalty to the parsonage gave birth to a puzzle, and a resentment, that God should choose to look down on his own pious station, the parsonage compound, from the profane heights of Itoko. There was of course the mystery of the Chief's stable with live horses near the crest of the hill, but beyond that, this dizzying road only sheered upwards from one noisy market to the other, looking down across Ibàràpa and Ita Aké into the most secret recesses of the parsonage itself. (*Aké* 1)

Why would God choose to look down upon the parsonage? The boy speculates that the Chief's horses might be an attraction. These comments combine a religious perspective on the landscape—in which elements in the landscape should correspond, particularly in their height, to their relative worthiness in God's eyes—with a boy's pragmatic assessment of the attractions of Itoko. Throughout the narrative, combinations of beliefs and perspectives, rather than conflicts between them, are used to reflect the child's ability to assimilate and live by the rules, values and assumptions of different cultures.

The narrative represents the world from the child's perspective. Following a marching band through the town when he is only four, Soyinka soon leaves behind the only part of town with which he is familiar: "Then the curious thing happened; after the bookseller's, the wall rolled away into a different area I had never seen before. Soon it moved away altogether, was covered up by houses and shops and disappeared for ever" (*Aké* 38). The boy attributes the movement to the wall itself; it is the wall which leaves him, not the other way around. In addition, Soyinka reveals the child's lack of fear at this point; he is only curious about these changes, not afraid of them.

Because Soyinka's parents are Christian, his world is filled with Christian symbolism. The orchard next to the Canon's house is "an extension of scripture classes, church lessons or sermons. A leaf-plant, mottled white-and-red was called the Cana lily. As Christ was nailed to the Cross and his wounds spurted blood, a few drops stuck to the leaves of the lily stigmatizing it forever" (*Aké* 2). The child accepts this explanation without question, but wonders what causes the white spots on the plant, and offers his own solution: "Perhaps it had to do with the washing of sins in the blood of Christ, leaving even the most mottled spots in a person's soul, snow-white" (2). He believes that the pomegranate is the fruit which tempted Eve in the Garden of Eden, even though the gardener of the orchard denies it: "We asked if it was *the* apple but Gardener only laughed and said No. Nor, he added, would that apple be found on the black man's soil" (3). While the child Soyinka pays no attention to this added comment, for the reader, it is an ominous sign of the divisions which threaten Soyinka's childhood vision of the world as unified, whole, and full of symbolic significance. Where the child sees the plants as directly related to Biblical events, the Gardener sees an absolute division because of race: nothing growing in the black man's soil could be from the Garden of Eden.

The child's world is also filled with the spirits of Yoruba religion. The forest, in particular, is associated with spirits; the Canon's home has its back turned "to the world of spirits and ghommids who inhabited the thick woods and chased home children who had wandered too deeply in them for firewood, mushrooms and snails" (*Aké* 2). These spirits, as well as Christian saints and miracles, are a part of his mother's stories to him: "No, there was no question about it, our Uncle Sanya was an *òrò;* Wild Christian had seen and heard proofs of it many times over" (11). In Achebe's novel, only one religious perspective will survive; here, Soyinka is able to assimilate both.

There are numerous examples of this unified point of view throughout *Aké*. For example, after hearing a story in which gourds break off from their moorings and chase a tortoise, Soyinka worries about the same thing happening to him: "I roved through the woods on the next expedition with one fearful eye on anything bulbous. . . . I saw them raining down on me, then pursuing me through the woods. If Wild Christian prayed hard enough, perhaps it could happen" (*Aké* 81-82). The African folk tale is merged with the Christian belief in the efficacy of prayer, particularly the prayers of pious Christians.

The child's unified worldview is threatened when he attends missionary schools. At one school, even the grass is divided: "Grass, ordinary smooth, green luscious grass which I had taken for granted on the lawns and playing-fields of Aké was now split into two categories—good, and bad" (*Aké* 170). The end result of such classification is a patchwork, as the boys are taught to pull up the "bad" grass: "Looking down from the upper floor of the building, the football field especially appeared to be under the attack of a fungoid growth or some other kind of communicable skin disease" (170). The destruction of the grass foreshadows the destruction of the child's fusion of Yoruba and Christian horizons as a result of the missionaries' insistence on the authority of the Christian horizon alone. The narrative ends: "It was time to commence the mental shifts for admittance to yet another irrational world of adults and their discipline" (230). The number of different beliefs and cultures which can be assimilated is limited; as the child is exposed to more "worlds," he is unable to retain his sense of the world's unity.

The loss of unity is exemplified by the adult Soyinka's response to the contemporary landscape. At certain points in the narrative, he describes the contemporary situation of Aké: "An evil thing has happened to Aké parsonage. The land is eroded, the lawns are bared and mystery driven from its once secretive combs. . . . The surviving houses, houses which formed the battlements of Aké parsonage are now packing cases on a depleted landscape, full of creaks, exposed and nerveless" (*Aké* 3-4). The loss of mystery, the "nervelessness" of the houses, all suggest that his unified vision of a living landscape is gone. Partly, this is the result of growing older: "Even the baobab has shrunk with time, yet I had imagined that this bulwark would be eternal, beyond the growing perspectives of a vanished childhood" (63). The town itself has also changed as a result of the intrusion of the West: "The dusty road which once grandly intervened between our backyard wall and the church wall is now shrunken; a half, pressed against St Peter's parsonage wall is shared among a variety of stores peddling the products of a global waste industry. . . . Along the same midnight walk of Dayisi the guitarist now darts the young hawker, releasing into the faces of passers-by through his finger on the caller's button, the dulcet chimes of Made-in-Hong-Kong doorbells" (149-150). The shrinking is literal—there is less space in the road—and spiritual; the village has shrunk because it no longer sees itself as at the center of the world. Instead, it lives on the waste of the industrial powers. It is not only the fact that Soyinka has grown up that makes his earlier vision of the world impossible to keep; the world itself has changed in ways which would prevent anyone from seeing it the way Soyinka was able to see his home town as a child. The nostalgia of the narrative, the sense of describing a lost world, is thus not merely a sentimental grasping at the lost innocence of childhood, but a more radical critique of present-day Nigeria: the country has lost its past, lost its dignity, and lost its unified vision of the world.

CHEIKH HAMIDOU KANE

Cheikh Hamidou Kane's *Ambiguous Adventure* is also concerned with the intrusion of the West into Africa, and the resulting crisis in traditional African societies. Kane, however, infuses his novel with a vision of the world based on Islamic beliefs that defines the significance and value of landscape description in very different terms. This difference emphasizes that landscape is not a single, given, "transparent" convention of the novel, as in Western narratives, but rather that it is part of an implied vision of the world. The conventional Western description of landscape encodes certain beliefs about nature, reality, and man's position in them which are redefined in Kane's Islamic novel.

Kane identifies the roots of this difference in a discussion between a Frenchman and an African Muslim, Samba Diallo's father, on their conceptions of the universe. Paul Lacroix says: "The earth is not flat. It has no steep slopes which give upon the abyss. The sun is not a candelabrum set upon a blue porcelain dais. The universe which science has revealed to the West is less immediately human, but confess that it is more solid" (Kane 75-76). It is this vision of the universe, or something like it, that establishes the function of landscape as primarily that of setting. It may serve some secondary purpose, such as reflecting the mood of the main character, but the description of landscape in literature is necessary, in this view, because it is part of the world of fact, of reality. Diallo's father, on the other hand, sees the visible world as only a small and insignificant part of an immense spiritual universe, and he responds to Lacroix as follows: "I know that you do not believe in the shade; nor in the end of the world. What you do not see does not exist. The moment, like a raft, carries you on the luminous circle of its round disc, and you deny the abyss that lies about you" (Kane 80). In this image, the visible world shrinks in importance: what is important is not the luminous disc—although it is beautiful—but the places between which it transports us.

In Sufi religious doctrine, the visible world participates in the being of God: "This world and all that is in it are reflections and theophanies of the Names and Qualities of God" (Seyyed Hossein Nasr, qtd. in Johnson, "Crescent and Consciousness" 248). However, it is a world of appearance, which can separate one from the reality of God. In Kenneth Harrow's reading of the novel, Diallo's spiritual teacher "stands for the other-worldly position of what Coulon calls *le marabout,* the spiritual leader who denies the primacy of the material values of the worldly ruler" (Harrow 287). As a result of this attitude towards the visible world, there are very few descriptions of landscape within the novel. Kane will often sketch in only the bare outline of a scene: "That evening, as he [Diallo's teacher] was silently praying at the door of his little cabin . . ." (Kane 24). In this example, the time of day is significant because it is the hour of prayer, and the "little cabin" suffices to remind the reader of the teacher's asceticism. Any further description would only focus the reader's attention on surface realities rather than staying attuned to the spiritual center of the narrative.

There are, however, other uses of land imagery in *Ambiguous Adventure*. The country is often used as a metaphor for its people, with the chief of the Diallobé and the teacher at its center. The Most Royal Lady says "My brother is the living heart of this country" (Kane 35). The religious leader and the king are the conscience and soul of the kingdom; leaving the land is like leaving a living body.

The end of the day, in this novel, is symbolically linked to the end of life, to death, and thus also to a closeness with God. The philosophical discussion between Lacroix and Diallo's father, for example, is inspired by a sunset that seems to foretell the end of the world: "Above the abyss the sun was suspended, dangerously. The liquid silver of its heat had been reabsorbed, without any loss of its light's splendor" (Kane 74). The language of this description, especially the abyss and the "dangerous suspension" of the sun, reinforce Diallo's father's vision that the world will someday come to an end, a vision that comforts him, as it suggests the end of division from God and the final revelation of truth. Looking at this dramatic sky, Lacroix wonders for a moment whether this Islamic belief in the end of the world is true. Thus the sky both symbolizes Diallo's father's belief, and influences Lacroix to question his own beliefs. Another example of the symbolic use of landscape is a twilight scene in which Samba Diallo is praying: "His long white caftan—turned violet now by the evening light—was swept through by a kind of shiver, which grew more pronounced in measure as the voice was rising. . . . To the east the sky was like an immense lilac-colored crystal" (60). As Kenneth Harrow claims, "Kane represents the moment of closest contact with the Divine by the evening prayer, the liminal moment when awareness . . . of what the Sufis call Reality or the Truth—attributes of God—is most sensibly felt" (Harrow 292). The robe is the color of the sky, and the movement of the caftan corresponds to the movement of Diallo's voice as he prays. These connections emphasize the unity of Diallo's spirit with God in the moment of prayer. The landscape is significant because it emphasizes the transcendental nature of prayer.

Having established this vision of the natural world as transitory appearance, significant only when it can be used to symbolize or illustrate spiritual insights, Kane shows the foreignness of the Western view of the world as objectified and "real." In Paris, Samba Diallo describes a street scene in radically objective terms; he sees "objects of flesh" and "objects of metal" (Kane 128). This takes the Western conventional description of setting to its extreme. People and automobiles are both merely objects, senselessly "congesting the streets" (128). The fool, the teacher's companion, also shares Samba Diallo's intuitive perception of Western objectivity: "On the hard carapace, there was only the clattering of a thousand hard shells. Had men no longer feet of flesh?" (91). These passages reveal the meaninglessness of a world described completely objectively, and suggest the alienation these characters feel in a world in which spiritual concerns receive so little attention.

In *Ambiguous Adventure* Samba Diallo occasionally identifies himself with nature: "Being Nature herself, I do not dare to fight against her" (Kane 140). This identification with nature is presented in contrast to the communist desire to subject nature: "You are fighting for her subjection" (139-140). Diallo's vision of nature is a product of his childhood: "In former times the world was like my father's dwelling: everything took me into the very essence of itself, as if nothing could exist except through me" (149). These passages imply that Kane is blending Islamic beliefs with traditional African relationships to nature, asserting that nature is appearance and yet having his main character identify himself with it. The world of nature and appearance, however, is not completely annihilated by Islamic belief. Okasha says that, for the Islamic artist, "God is at the heart of all existence . . . [he is] the appearance and the reality hidden behind it" (Okasha 14). Thus there need be no division between appearance and reality as long as meditating on appearance leads to the divine.

In the end, Samba Diallo rejects the world of appearance. In a dialogue after his death, Diallo's spirit is asked if he will regret leaving behind the illusions of the world of appearance, and he replies, "I wish for you" (Kane 175). Appearance is rejected in favor of truth. By including this dialogue, the novel itself moves beyond the world of appearance; there is no landscape here, no setting, only disembodied voices. In moving into this spiritual realm, the novel leaves behind the social and political problems that have been raised throughout the novel. While the ending fits the Islamic code of the novel, by moving into the spiritual world it leaves the desperate situation of Diallo's country unchanged.

CONCLUSIONS AND POSTINDEPENDENCE NOVELS

In each of these texts, *The Palm-Wine Drinkard*, *Things Fall Apart*, *Aké*, and *Ambiguous Adventure*, land imagery is used to reveal the religious horizons of the text. Achebe, Soyinka, and Kane also trace in their narratives the destruction caused by the intrusion of the West into Africa. The authors use landscape to convey to the reader the perceptual differences between Islam, Christianity, and traditional African religions and dramatize the conflicts between worldviews that arise in colonial periods. Achebe is the most conventional of these authors in his use of landscape, while Soyinka and Kane experiment with radically subjective perceptions of the land. Of these two, Kane provides a unified, consistent and finally all-encompassing Islamic worldview that denies the importance of the world of appearance. While in Kane's novel Diallo escapes from the difficulties of the material world into a realm of pure spirit, Soyinka's autobiography traces the changes in his perception of the world as he assimilates new truths and beliefs. In addition, Soyinka is able to explain the disintegration of his unified worldview confronted by the Westernization of Nigeria; both he himself and the land have changed irreparably. Most disturbing of the three, Achebe's novel ends with the shadow of an inevitable conflict on the horizon, as the accommodating middle space of the narrative disappears.

While each of the previously discussed texts focuses on the colonial period in West Africa, there is also a growing body of literature situated in postindependence Africa. Many of these works, such as Ayi Kwei Armah's *The Beautyful Ones Are Not Yet Born*, Kofi Awoonor's *This Earth, My Brother* and Cyprian Ekwensi's *Jagua Nana* are set in an urban environment, reflecting the rapid urbanization of Africa. Armah's fiction especially documents the disillusionment of the post-independence period resulting from government and private corruption, using images of a decaying urban environment:

For years and years the buildings had been plastered at irregular intervals with paint and with distemper, mostly of an official murk-yellow color. In the intervals, between successive layers of distemper, the walls were caressed and thoroughly smothered by brown dust blowing off the roadside together with swirling grit from the coal and gravel of the railroad yard within and behind, and the corners of walls where people passed always dripped with the engine grease left by thousands of transient hands. Every new coating, then, was received as just another inevitable accretion in a continuing story whose beginnings were now lost and whose end no one was likely to bother about. (Armah 11)

In this passage from *The Beautyful Ones Are Not Yet Born*, Armah shows a smooth transition between the colonial and postcolonial periods—even the "official" color doesn't change, as new layers are painted on over the old. There is no fundamental change, only "accretion." In this description, the dirt and grime are created by natural causes (the wind and dust), by industry (the coal yard), by government (the murk-yellow distemper) and by urban workers, who leave a trail of engine grease on the walls. This last effect is one that Armah uses often, showing the marks left by people's bodies on walls, stairways, and latrines. These marks, like graffiti, are a record of their passage, their human presence in the city. Unlike graffiti, however, the marks are the result of grimy jobs (engine grease) and lack of access to running water. They are the marks of people being debased and oppressed by their environment. Armah has perhaps been the most vivid and outspoken in his depiction of the degrading environment of the urban proletariat, but others have followed, showing the correlations between social and physical environments. Both Achebe and Soyinka, for example, have written novels with postcolonial urban settings, although their focus has been on the urban educated elite.

All of the writers above are part of a generation spanning both colonial and postcolonial Africa. Now, a new generation of writers is appearing in Africa. Ben Okri, a Nigerian writer living in Britain, has published several novels and a collection of short stories set primarily in Lagos. Okri's vision of Lagos shares some similarities with Armah's visions of Accra: both document the filth and slime of the streets of the city, and the decay of buildings and roads. However, in Okri's *The Landscapes Within*, the mysteries, frustration, corruption, and filth of everyday life are connected to the actions of individuals. The main character, Omovo, is a painter, whose works reveal the inner landscapes of his thought. He works in an office, however, where everyone participates in the Nigerian system of "one hand washing the other"; Omovo's refusal of a bribe results in his dismissal from the firm. Disoriented and lost in a Lagos park at night, Omovo and Keme stumble across the mutilated body of a young girl; when the police arrive, the body has disappeared. In each case, people are at work, not solely market forces or the oppression of international capitalism.

In Okri's novels, Nigeria, Lagos, individual neighborhoods, and homes are seen as human productions, created for specific needs and desires, and thus potentially capable of being re-formed and re-imagined. The possibility of transformation sets Okri's urban landscapes apart from Armah's apocalyptic visions, and suggests a new direction for future West African literature.

West African literature by men tends to focus on the outside world: the village, the bush, the streets of Lagos. Compared to literature by women, there are fewer images of interiors. There is also a stronger interest in the nation, although it is usually a background to a smaller geographic horizon, such as the seven villages of Umuofia or the city of Lagos. These characteristics reflect the greater freedom of movement of West African men and the much greater chance that an educated man might have an opportunity to participate in governing the nation.

Each narrative's setting, and the circumstances of its male protagonist, create different resolutions for the question of the relative significance of individual freedom and communal (or national) responsibility. Achebe's Okonkwo suggests that individual freedom is impossible without community, while in *Aké*, Soyinka seems to warn that the child's ability to conceive of a united, integrated community will be destroyed by his impending Western education. Kane's Diallo moves beyond nationalism and national responsibility to a metaphysical, spiritual resolution, while Tutuola's narrator tells his fearful, individual adventures to his audience, after he has safely returned to his community—the frame of his narrative is the community. Ben Okri's *The Landscapes Within* suggests that a community without individual freedom will slowly destroy itself; Okri's young characters leave the country, taking their talents with them.

Each of these writers also sets his work within a larger, international horizon, tracing the influence of international forces within the nation. Colonial education, Christianity, Islam, and multinationals have all changed the landscapes of West Africa. By tracing these changes, West African writers reveal the continuing connections between West Africa and the rest of the world; they mourn for what has been lost and pose the question of who benefits from the maintenance of these connections. Because of these international influences, the landscape has changed, and the worldview of West Africans has been transformed. Through their narratives, these West African writers reveal that the horizon of individuals in West Africa has been expanded, perforce, to encompass the world.

NOTE

1. Another aspect of this controversy for Nigerian critics was Tutuola's use of D.

Chapter 4

"In the Land of a Dying Illusion": The Landscape of Black South African Township Novels

For black[1] South African writers, there is a special urgency to describe the country from their own perspective, to make the lives and aspirations of their people visible, and to bring to light the intolerable conditions in which they live. Through their work, the entire landscape of South Africa becomes visible for the first time.

Novels by black South African writers are different from those by other sub-Saharan novelists. Apartheid changed the political landscape; blacks were herded into townships and homelands, seeing the wealth of South Africa but barred from living in the white areas or having the luxuries they supplied for others.

The homelands were a part of this overall policy, identifying each black in South Africa as a member of a particular ethnic group, and then assigning him or her to a "homeland." While blacks accounted for 68.4% of the population in South Africa, they were allotted less than 14% of the total land area of South Africa for their "homelands" (July 554-555). Throughout the twentieth century black South Africans were forcibly removed from urban and suburban areas and transported to remote rural areas with no industry or other source of employment. In this way, the homelands served as a reserve of migrant labor; when needed, workers were recruited and brought back into urban and industrial areas, but as soon as they were unnecessary, they were returned to the homelands. Thus the homelands policy led to the prolonged separation of families; Soweto became filled with hostels for men, while women in the homelands struggled to support their families on subsistence farming and occasional checks from their husbands. While the laws, policies and terminology of the South African government changed gradually over the years, the ideology of apartheid remained; black South

Africans were consistently denied equal opportunities and rights under the law. This constant pressure on the African community had several ramifications.

Culturally, apartheid created a situation in which many black writers were suspicious of those who would urge them to "return to their roots," as this was an argument for the oppression of blacks under the policy of separate development. In particular, when Négritude gained popularity in the rest of sub-Saharan Africa as a form of appreciation for black aesthetics and traditional African dance, storytelling and myth, South African writers responded with skepticism:

I am a product of cultural cross-impacts, having lived with whites, Indians and colored people all my life in South Africa. These must exercise a tremendous influence on my art. If there is any Negro-ness in it—as there is bound to be if my tone is not false— why should I get excited about it and formulate philosophic statements about the fact? (Mphahlele, "The Importance" 11)

While black South African writers value African traditions as part of their contemporary community's culture, many have denied that there is a virtue in racial purity, or that there is a racial difference that is essential rather than culturally created. In addition, Mphahlele and others have been suspicious about over-romanticizing the African past, because it can serve as a way of avoiding commitment in the present: "While we try to re-establish our past, such a function can only find proper focus if it is going to help us know ourselves better in the context of present-day cultural activity" (Mphahlele, qtd. in Bishop 104[2]). An exploration of the African past may be only a romantic escape, unless it is linked to a vision of the needs and desires of the contemporary society.

In addition to these concerns about romanticizing traditional African culture, black South Africans have developed a distinct body of criticism on the significance and function of literature: "The South African writer must continue in a stage of commitment to the revolution that must come" (Mphahlele, qtd. in Bishop 120); "In the new nations, as well as the areas still under alien domination, the artist and writer has the historic task of witnessing and communicating the new African culture emerging from the liberation struggles" (Chima, qtd. in Bishop 123). In black South African literature, characters may preach to their audience, endorsing particular paths of action: "They thought that they had reduced us to *untermenschen* but they lied. We are living proof that they lied. We must always tell our story to our children and to our children's children" (Rive 197). Such passages reveal the intensity of the writer's identification with his community's struggle for freedom from oppression, and suggest that the goal of much of black South African writing has been to achieve political and social changes rather than solely to create great works of fiction.

While black South African writers have criticized other Africans for being too romantic in their descriptions of Africa, South African literature has been criticized for being too politicized and predictable:

What we do get from South Africa . . . is journalistic fact, parading outrageously as imaginative literature. We find here a type of fiction which exploits the ready-made plots of racial violence, social apartheid, interracial love affairs which are doomed from the beginning, without any attempt to transcend or transmute these given "social facts" into artistically persuasive works of fiction. (Nkosi , qtd. in Asein 207)

Lewis Nkosi's critique of the journalistic qualities of black South African fiction was a significant criticism of the plots of many stories from the 1950s and 1960s, but it overlooks the ways in which many South African stories did transform the landscape of South Africa, using descriptions of townships, homelands, farms, and cities to unveil the boundaries and divisions that apartheid inscribed on the land. As Sam Asein has said,

[Although] the non-white South African novelist, it does become clear, like any other writer can hardly divorce his creative sensibility from the overpowering facts of his environment without falsifying his external social reality. . . . the setting in the South African novel is more often than not enriched with a symbolic value and function in the total fictional realization, defining as is very often the case the limits of thematic reference and the depth of characterization. (Asein 208-209)

The landscape of South African fiction is not only scarred by apartheid, but is also marked symbolically, revealing the political, religious, and communal horizons of the texts.

   In this chapter, I read descriptions of landscape in black South African fiction by men; in the following chapter, I consider the significance of landscape in works by Miriam Tlali and Bessie Head. The gendered nature of literature by men has often been invisible; many books on the African novel or African literature have failed to include even one woman author, yet these studies have not overtly considered the effects of masculine identity on male writing. In this chapter, I hope to establish some of the conventions of black male descriptions of the South African landscape, in order to reveal the differences between their work and that of women from South Africa in the next chapter.

TOWNSHIP LITERATURE

In South African literature, there is a tension between describing the vitality of the black community and avoiding any suggestion that the policies which forced the creation of this separate community are acceptable. The locus of this tension is most often the township, the residential area set apart for blacks near urban centers. Township literature describes the experience of life in these restricted areas, providing not only a realistic setting for their narratives but also a compelling argument for the end of racial segregation and domination through their descriptions of the horrors of the townships.

   Since World War II, South Africa's township populations have exploded. They are huge ghettos, ringing the major cities with high density residential areas. Every day there is a mass exodus out of the townships and into the city, where the jobs are; many have to commute for over an hour each way. The townships are much larger than the cities they support: Soweto has a million more people living in it than Johannesburg, and it is only one of the townships that surround that city. Within Soweto, there are gradations of wealth; a few pockets of middle-class housing exists for those who have managed to become businessmen, lawyers, doctors, or ministers. These are surrounded by vast collections of small one-family homes, typically housing eight to ten people in two rooms, which in turn are a step up from the shacks of the shantytowns within Soweto, made out of petrol tins, cardboard, and plastic, housing thousands who cannot find other shelter, and the dormitories housing single men and husbands forced to live apart from their families in the homelands.

While the townships of South Africa suffer under slum conditions, the formerly all-white areas are gleaming: neat bungalows set back from the streets in the suburbs, and towers of glass in the cities. The contrast between the two is inescapable; under apartheid, black South Africans moved between these extremes every day, emphasizing the contrast between their lives and the lives of white South Africans.

In describing white-owned locations, black writers often provided specifically visual landscapes, presenting these places as antiseptic and inhuman:

"Mind the wall girls," the general manager warned from behind an acre of gleaming mahogany with gilded ballpens jutting out of a cobalt blue stand, two scarlet and cream-white telephones and a brown leather table mat on top. The off-white walls of the spacious room would embarrass a fly, and the ankle-deep ocean-green carpet appeared not to have been made with a view to being trodden underfoot. (Matshoba, "A Son of the First Generation" 75)

The materials of the office do not seem intended for human use but rather intimidate and repel the girls, an impression reinforced by the manager's warning "mind the wall." This space is designed not to receive or record the mark of their presence but to deny it: the carpet appears not to be made for feet to walk on. This luxurious space is clearly reserved for whites only.

Occasionally, black South African writers romanticized rural life, particularly rural areas where there were few or no white settlers:

The huts were methodically grouped together. The groups were neatly spaced and protected a whole family of families. They were a community. They belonged together. Their cows and their goats, their chickens and their pigs, their horses and their mules were nearby in separate areas. . . . Beautiful tropical trees abounded. The tilled areas provided mealies and sweet potatoes. There was plenty of fish in the Umgeni and the Umzinyathi, and game to hunt in the unspoiled bush. (Ramgobin 5)

This is an Africa before the fall. The emphasis is on harmony, plenty, and simplicity. This description comes dangerously close to a wistful desire to return to a nontechnological society. Dangerous, because it is this life that the South African government held up as the promise of the so-called homelands and that it used as an excuse to undereducate the African population. For these reasons, most black South African writers who described the homelands were careful to reveal that these were not rural paradises:

The soil was red, ironically reminding me of Avalon and Doornkop cemeteries back home, the land parched and scarred with erosion. In the first fields that we passed the maize had grown hardly a metre high. The weeds, blackjack outstanding, outgrew it. A woman in dusty traditional attire with a baby strapped to her back . . . was searching for stems that might have been overlooked at harvest time. (Matshoba, "Three Days in the Land of a Dying Illusion" 158)

The harsh reality of rural poverty in the Transkei is illustrated here, underlined by the parallel with the red dirt of the cemetery and the use of the phrase "might have been"; there is no certainty that the woman will even find the meager scraps she seeks.

The most prominent fact of black South Africans' relations to their contemporary environment under apartheid was the lack of choice about where they could live and work. They were forced to come to terms with environments they did not choose, and to which they had no familial or ethnic ties. Both the homelands and the townships were creations of the minority government in South Africa, and both served their purposes.

Despite this fact, however, black South African writers showed that within these locations black communities formed that were supportive and productive, creating bonds to each other in spite of the grimness of their surroundings. In township literature this sense of community is the necessary foundation for revolution and resistance in South Africa.

ALEX LA GUMA

Alex La Guma's novella "A Walk in the Night" is a grim, naturalistic tale of life in the Coloured township of District Six in Cape Town. We follow the wanderings of Michael Adonis, a worker who has just been fired, as he moves among the streets, cafes and apartments of the district. We also follow the actions of other characters: Willieboy, Constable Raalt, and Frankie Lorenzo, whose movements, combined with Adonis', create a vision of the social and physical landscape of District Six.

Alex La Guma is one of the few African writers whose attention to the physical landscape of his fiction has been noted and discussed critically:

The function of La Guma's settings is not primarily to give verisimilitude to the moral progress of his characters. Nor is it to create, in Lukac's conception, a 'totality of objects' through which the protagonist must struggle in order to gain an authentic sense of self. . . . The surface of slum life in an under-developed country differs from that of civil society, in being not a veneer, but the most direct expression of the quality of that life. (Rabkin 57-58).

La Guma's District Six has been called the main protagonist of the novel (Green 13); La Guma focuses on the interrelated landscapes of District Six, rather than the experiences and emotions of specific individuals. The structure of the story itself reinforces La Guma's emphasis on spatial relations rather than individual plots. The narrative shifts from character to character as they pass each other in the street; in the final sections of the novel, the only connection between scenes is that they are all happening simultaneously. While most critics see this form as simply a device to emphasize the naturalism of his story, William Carpenter sees this "spatial form" (Carpenter 4) as integrally related to the collective consciousness created by the novel.

La Guma's descriptions of the township District Six in "A Walk in the Night" suggest a postapocalyptic world:

He turned down another street, away from the artificial glare of Hanover, between stretches of damp, battered houses with their broken-ribs of front-railings; cracked walls and high tenements that rose like the leftovers of a bombed area in the twilight; vacant lots and weed-grown patches where houses had once stood. . . .   In some of the doorways people sat or stood, murmuring idly in the fast-fading light like wasted ghosts in a plague-ridden city. (La Guma 19)

The decrepitude of the buildings, and the feeling of a place that has been battered and broken by too much use and too little repair, is relentlessly communicated. It is an environment which envelops those who inhabit it, providing little of the objective distance suggested by a purely visual description. In addition, the impressionistic approach to description used in the examples above adds to the sense of an observer in the streets, feeling and smelling the things he describes rather than merely recording them.

J.M. Coetzee, in his essay "Man's Fate in the Novels of Alex La Guma," criticizes the lack of objective distance in La Guma's descriptive passages:

". . . an *old* iron bed. . . *unwashed* bedding. . . a *backless* chair. . .   a *chipped* ashtray. . .   cigarette *butts*. . . *burnt* matches. . ." —everything named is named with its own gesture of repudiation. The significance of the passage is not a room and its details, but rather (a) a room, plus (b) the horror of the room. . . .   La Guma's world, so overflowing with things, is nonetheless not an objective world, for the things themselves are overflowing with the writer's subjectivity. ("Man's Fate" 22, Coetzee's italics.)

These catalogues of decrepit, decaying objects, Coetzee claims, express "a revulsion which must confess in places to being merely fastidious" ("Man's Fate" 23). Yet these passages also have "a more interesting side": "A repetitiousness that becomes excessive and even obsessive, the testament of one man's horror of a degraded world" ("Man's Fate" 23).

In this environment, people are often represented as objects, simply a part of the landscape: "He continued to remain something less than nondescript, part of the blurred face of the crowd, inconspicuous as a smudge on a grimy wall" (La Guma 69). The environment seems to be a naturalist prison from which there is no escape; even a cockroach is accorded its own paragraph, suggesting an equality between its life and that of the characters: "The cockroach paused over the stickiness and a creaking of boards somewhere startled it. . . . After a while the room was silent again and it returned and commenced to gorge itself" (La Guma 91). Are the characters as driven by their own needs, as helpless to alter their environment, as the roach?

Coetzee sees these details as evidence of the novel's naturalism: "At the end of the book we are back nearly where we started. . . . a 'basically static approach to reality' belongs to the naturalistic novel" ("Man's Fate" 19). The possibility of change and development lies not in the lives and minds of his characters, but "in his reader's synthesizing intelligence, as it puts together the elements of a pattern too scattered for the characters to perceive" ("Man's Fate" 19). Coetzee finds this solution to the difficulties of realistic portrayal of township life unsuccessful, because of "the gulf it establishes between life and the intelligence that makes order of life" ("Man's Fate" 20). If the pattern only emerges for the outside observer, Coetzee implies, it will not be possible for those within the system to interpret their situation correctly.

Yet there are some hopeful images within the novel itself. Particularly images of the ocean, associated most strongly with the figure of Joe, offer, as Adrian Roscoe claims, "a relief from human ugliness" (*Uhuru's Fire* 238): "In the rock pools [Joe] would examine the mysterious life of the sea things, the transparent beauty of starfish and anemone, and hear the relentless, consistent pounding of the creaming waves against the granite citadels of rock" (La Guma 91). Roscoe sees this as an "almost Wordsworthian solution," (*Uhuru's Fire* 238) yet again using a European standard for the analysis of African landscape description. However, this vision of Joe's life on the beach is situated within a larger social and political horizon which clearly limits the possibility of redemption within the natural world. The redemptive value of these experiences for Joe can only be temporary: we know that the beaches are soon going to be closed to non-whites. In addition, the last phrase echoes a previous image in the novel, in which a crowd's muttering is described as "The mutter of dark water eroding the granite cliffs, sucking at the sand-filled cracks and dissolving the banks of clay" (La Guma 83). This image reverses the ideology of naturalism. Rather than simply depicting humanity worn and oppressed by the forces of industrialized society, La Guma includes in his novel a counterimage in which the crowds of humanity will eventually wear away the citadel of rock which oppresses it. In contrast to Wordsworth, however, the sea is only a metaphor for the persistence and determination of the people; nature alone offers no solution to the problems of District Six.

William Carpenter sees the muttering of the crowd as a "scene of representation:"

La Guma marks off this 'scene of representation' from the ambient representation . . . first by unifying the voices of the bystanders under the image of the ocean, as if the people united were a natural force, and then by presenting their responses as anonymous, and therefore typical or general. . . . the readers and author witness the creation of a collective consciousness of significance, both the crowd's and their own. (Carpenter 3)

If this is the founding moment of the crowd's collective consciousness, then La Guma has included the possibility of change and development within the story of the novel. Rather than seeing the synthesis of the pattern of oppression as occurring solely within the reader's imagination, as Coetzee does, Carpenter suggests that La Guma evokes a collective consciousness that includes the reader: "Still writing and publishing in Africa, La Guma could still feel that his novel would propagate the collective consciousness it embodied in South Africa itself" (Carpenter 16). The image of the crowd as ocean, witnessed by the reader, extends the horizon of the novel beyond its fictional frame and into the spatial and temporal frame of the reader.

RICHARD RIVE

Richard Rive's *Buckingham Palace: District Six* is a novel of the townships, but also of remembrance, commemorating the community of District Six in Cape Town, which was destroyed to make room for white development. His novel, in contrast to La Guma's, deliberately sets out to commemorate the community of District Six, its values and humanity.

The novel opens:

I remember
those who used to live in District Six, those who lived in Caledon Street and Clifton Hill and busy Hanover Street. There are those of us who still remember the ripe, warm days. Some of us still romanticise and regret when our eyes travel beyond the dead bricks and split treestumps and wind-tossed sand. (Rive 1)

This opening is an invocation of the place, "calling" it into being. Rive's purpose is to celebrate the life of the community rather than emphasize its degraded surroundings.

The playfulness of the community is both childlike and revolutionary. "Buckingham Palace" is the name of a small street of houses in District Six. The history of the name is unknown, but it serves as a starting point of identity; when Pretty-Boy decides to name his house, he chooses "Windsor Park." These names not only silently point up the contrast between the luxury of the royal palace in England and the poverty of District Six, but also reveal the actual connections between the two locations; as part of the British Empire, South Africa has also been exploited for the wealth of England. The two Buckingham Palaces are linked by the history of imperialism.

Zoot and Pretty-Boy's house is gradually transformed from a gutted out shell to a livable domestic environment. They acquire a bed, chairs, and a table, and then more expensive equipment: a refrigerator, a stove, and a radio. These objects are all scavenged or stolen, but in their middle-class domesticity represent the desire of the loosely connected group of men who live there not to be outcasts but to be members of the community. It is ironic that it is only by going out-side the law that they can fulfill middle-class desires generated by living on the fringes of South African society.

Everything is slightly off kilter: the house is newly painted, but bright pink, and the painters have painted everything else pink, including the bed, the stove, the refrigerator, and the radio. The house name is on a sign, but spelled "Winsor Park." These quirks reveal the makeshift nature of their domestic ar-rangements; while replicating stable middle-class patterns, the association of people here is only temporary. Each of them will move in and out as they find work or love, or are arrested or in trouble. The power of the novel is in repre-senting the efforts of a community to form a unified front with no roots or long-term relations to tie them together.

During the course of the novel, the entire District is condemned, and resi-dents are offered homes elsewhere if they sign agreements to give up their homes in District Six. Those who trust the government and move out find themselves relocated farther away from Cape Town, in districts where the buildings have been put up so rapidly they are already decaying, and where there is no sense of community to prevent neighbors from robbing and harming each other. Those who stay watch the gradual emptying of their neighborhood:

Few children still played in the streets and fewer made their precarious ways over the scarred land. Their parents stayed indoors waiting for the notices to come, for the final axe to fall. And they closed their doors, shut their windows and drew down the blinds on their premature night and on the District that died before its death. (Rive 130-131)

Unlike some township novels, which create a binary world of black and white, Rive's novel of District Six portrays the gray areas: the colored, mixed-race, and Indian populations, mixing at times with both the whites and the Africans. The novel presents an image of an interracial group working together on a common (though futile) cause, trying to find a way to resist the evictions. Even the Jew-ish landlord, often a stock character of greed and exploitation in South African novels, is portrayed sympathetically, drawing connections to his own persecu-tion as a Jew in World War II and vowing to support the township residents in their resistance. The novel ends on a vision of future harmony between the op-pressors and the oppressed; standing on the rubble of Buckingham Palace, Zoot proclaims:

We knew that District Six was dirty and rotten. Their newspapers told us so often enough. But what they didn't say was that it was also warm and friendly. That it con-tained humans. That it was never a place-that it was a people. ... I promise you that our children and the children of those who are doing this to us, will join together and they will see that this will never happen again. (Rive 197-198)

By transforming geography into ethnography, Rive triumphantly "pits his little people and the value of their communal sense against the might of Apartheid's bulldozers" (Daymond, "The Lost Community" 19). The bulldozers can destroy the physical buildings and geography of District Six, but if the sense of community and solidarity is rooted, not in a place, but in a people, it will not be destroyed. His nostalgia for a place has been transformed into a praise poem for the people.

MONGANE SEROTE

Mongane "Wally" Serote is both a poet and a novelist; in addition, he is currently a member of the National Assembly in South Africa. In his poetry, Serote's landscapes tend towards the archetypal and symbolic, but in his novel *To Every Birth Its Blood*, he provides the reader with a vivid, realistic image of the township of Alexandra, outside Johannesburg.

In describing the township, Serote uses the simple present or past tense, providing a sense of immediacy: "Today is a Monday. It was a Monday night. There was, what was it? There was smoke coming out of the hundreds and hundreds of chimneys of Alexandra. . . . It felt like Mondays always do, as if it were the beginning of the world" (Serote 23). The details of this scene are not specific to a single evening; every Monday night is like this. Serote describes the lack of individuality of the people in the crowds; they are described as "hasty footsteps" (Serote 23) and voices, not as complete persons. Serote is sounding a common theme here: the dehumanization of blacks created by the pressures of apartheid. Yet the overall impression of this scene is one of life and energy: people flowing, voices sailing; Tsi, Serote's narrator here, sees it "as if it were the beginning of the world."

In Part I of the novel, we follow Tsi through the landscape of his life. He opens the novel with the premonition of an argument: "So, when she and I walked into the house after we had been in the street so long, I knew that another time was coming when we would have to be in the street again" (Serote 7). Throughout Part I, Tsi's restlessness drives him out of the house; he can only stay within the interior landscape if he is at peace with himself and with the others within the house. This opening raises the question of what the house represents. Tsi is always aware that the house is only provisionally theirs, both because blacks are not allowed to own property and because the rent is paid by his wife. Part of the ongoing argument between Tsi and his wife is his reluctance to pay his permit, which officially allows him to live in Alexandra. All of these factors affect Tsi's experience of life in the township, making it difficult for him to find a place for himself within the township that is not personally humiliating.

Tsi moves through the streets easily, looking for the faces of friends in the flow of the crowds. He drinks at *shebeens*, drops in at friends' houses, and traces his way through the neighborhoods of Alexandra. This pattern of movement is primarily male; the women he knows, his mother, his wife, and his mistress, are encountered only within their homes. Tsi moves between them, bringing his preoccupations and restlessness into their settings, hoping to be soothed and reassured yet certain that this is impossible.

Tsi is a journalist working for a white-owned paper in Johannesburg. On assignment with his colleague Boykie, Tsi experiences the larger landscape of South Africa as both beautiful and imprisoning, as his reveries about the land are interrupted by police roadblocks. He and Boykie are stopped and beaten by police; when they try to report it at a police station, they are beaten again and imprisoned.

Tsi describes the police station, completely integrating sights, sounds, and smells with the history of the place and the terror of the present moment:

A mixture of deodorant smells and paper, tobacco, old furniture, turned into a single smell, which characterizes all the places whose functions are proclaimed by notices, where warnings burden walls, counters and filing cabinets, where the sweat, tears, vomit and blood of many many people, who came and went, who never made it out of the doors, leave their spirits hanging in the air, which can never ever be cleaned. All these seemed to sing, seemed to whisper, seemed to warn us about where we were. ... There was going to be a display of power. (Serote 53)

In this description, Serote shows Tsi feeling the presence, not just of police power, but of the spirits of other people hanging in the air. Throughout the novel, Tsi and other characters feel the presence of the dead supporting them, comforting them, or challenging them. Thus Serote embodies his characters' beliefs in the role and importance of the ancestors within a contemporary environment.

Trying to prevent himself from breaking down under torture, Tsi recalls his grandmother's admonition that he was "like the plants, so merged with the soil and water, and wind, and the sun and the moon" (Serote 54). This imagery integrates Tsi with the land itself; his birth was a unification of the natural and spiritual powers of the land. After he is released from the prison cell, Tsi looks at the passing landscape: "The vastness, the emptiness, the horizons, the blue, blue sky, everything seemed to want to know, 'What have you learnt?'" (Serote 55). Throughout Part I, Tsi has resisted becoming a part of the Movement, trying to solve his restlessness, his dissatisfaction, through drinking, sex, or aimless roaming. Now he feels challenged by the land itself to respond to what has happened. From this point on, Tsi moves towards the Movement and active opposition to apartheid. His political, subversive activities are based both on the brutality he is forced to experience and on his identification with the land and the spirits of those who have died.

In Part I, Tsi is seen several times in cemeteries. In the first such scene, he turns in at the gate of the cemetery to sit on the grave of his grandfather. The graveyard, rather than being the classic, melancholy spot of Victorian novels, is a family gathering place; families assert their unity and continuity by coming to care for the graves of their relatives. Serote emphasizes this point through Tsi's encounter with an old man, a friend of his father's. Tsi greets him carefully and respectfully. The placement of this scene suggests a continuum between the living and the dead through the succession of generations. Thus Tsi has been born from the land and will die into it. His ties to the earth are strengthened by his awareness of his ancestors and the spirits of his people speaking to him through the landscape of South Africa. Against this landscape, the monuments of white colonial power in South Africa seem temporary obstructions.

In Part II of his novel, Serote broadens his canvas, describing the activities of several members of the Movement, both within Alexandra and in other parts of the country. The Movement itself is seen as spreading throughout the land: "A force which was slowly, very slowly but very systematically, like water flowing from a dam, approaching every corner of the country" (Serote 153). This aspect of Serote's description has been criticized by Martin Trump: "All disparities, all discordances are subsumed into Serote's organic images of the movement" (Trump 42). The Movement further absorbs the characters into itself: "The author appears to believe that the Movement, the political struggle against apartheid, the oppressed community and the individual committed to combatting apartheid are entirely synonymous, acting within the text as virtual tropes for each other" (Sole 72). Despite these difficulties, the organic images of the Movement as the wind, as water, as a gigantic tree, are part of Serote's project to broaden the horizon of his novel beyond the confines of Alexandra and Johannesburg. The Movement, the principal character of the second part of the novel, is followed as its members move through South Africa, Botswana, and Mozambique.

In this second part of the novel, Serote shows women's participation in the Movement as equals. Their participation is not limited to the support of men's efforts; they drive getaway cars, and plant bombs. While in the first part of the novel, we see Tsi trying to use women as supports and comfort, trying to find a base from which he can move out into the streets of Alexandra, here women themselves move out into the wider landscape. Oni and Dikeledi are both depicted expertly driving cars, a sign of their ability to move confidently around the country. Oni's movements, like those of the other members of the Movement, become mysterious and wide-ranging: "She closed the door behind her and disappeared into the dark. Before daybreak, she had reached Derdepoort. Three days later she was back in Walmanstadt" (Serote 201). The novel's representation of women carefully reflects the ideology of equality espoused by the Movement.

Kelwyn Sole, in his essay, "'This Time Set Again:' The Temporal and Political Conceptions of Serote's *To Every Birth Its Blood*," identifies two "logics" in the novel, the "poetic-symbolic" and the "realist-mimetic" (Sole 76). Neither logic is completely realized, as the two modes conflict and interfere with each other. Nowhere is this more apparent than in the difficulties of the ending of the novel.

At the end of the novel, Tsi is in exile. Alexandra, the place within which Tsi had an identity and a place, has receded into the distance; without that location, Tsi is "a stranger everywhere and forever" (Serote 195). In this foreign space, men and women in exile, including Yao, seek to 'ground' themselves through sexual relationships: "Men and women got so close that only the sharpest blade could pass between them. Yet they were so far from each other that even the ocean could not fill the gap" (196). Emotional distance is imagined as an infinite space; their search for closeness is doomed to failure, as each individual is experiencing a distance, a strangeness, within him or herself which prevents physical closeness in exile from becoming the emotional closeness of relationship.

Tsi overcomes this sense of distance through his faith that his exile will be only temporary. The novel ends with an image of a woman in the last stages of labor; a nurse bends over her, saying, "Push, push, push" (Serote 206), words which are repeated in the last words of the novel. The violence in the novel becomes transformed into the necessary, but not life-threatening, blood of birth; Tsi, in exile, must wait out his time, like a father waiting for a birth. The primary male character of Part I is now relegated to a secondary, passive role in the Movement, waiting for the next stage of the journey. Kelwyn Sole, reading this ending, finds it uncertain and disjointed, "final evidence of the paradoxical temporal character of a text whose thematic and narrative closure is in a very real sense incomplete" (Sole 69). Yet, reading the text as "poetic-symbolic" rather than "realist-mimetic," there is a sense of closure in the description of exile as a kind of waiting room, a limbo between the present and the future. It is also particularly suited to a description of men in exile, waiting to see what their actions in the past will bring to birth in South Africa.

CONCLUSION

All three of these novels attempt in different ways to reform the traditional Western novel, with its emphasis on individuality, to reflect a more communal or collective vision of society. In each, the description of the landscape inhabited by the characters is an intimate part of the author's project, revealing the characters' common oppression in the degrading surroundings of the townships. All three authors also emphasize life on the streets of the township: Michael Adonis, Zoot and Pretty-Boy, Tsi and Yao establish their identities and reinforce their ties with others through interactions on the street. Because these novels take place during the period of apartheid in South Africa, the streets of the townships are a significant public space for the black and Coloured communities. Despite their decrepit condition, the streets provide a (primarily) non-white space within which the people can express their communal roles and identify themselves as individuals within that communal space. The role of street life in forming a sense of self for characters in mens' novels is in strong contrast to the works of women writers, including women writers from South Africa, who emphasize the importance of interior spaces of the home and the workplace. Although Buchi Emecheta, Miriam Tlali, and other women writers occasionally describe street life, their characters define themselves by their more intimate relationships with family and friends, revealed through interactions within the home or workplace.

In each work, the author also broadens his horizon beyond the limits of the township. We see this in La Guma's image of the ocean; Rive's image of the community as a people, not a place; and Serote's image of Tsi's communion with the land. Each work finds an imaginative relationship to the landscape of South Africa that triumphs over the oppressive conditions of life for blacks in

South Africa. The degrading world of the townships and the immediate presence of the oppression of apartheid are mitigated by a horizon which includes a broader understanding of geography, and a broader dimension of time, looking back to a past and forward to a future in which apartheid was not, and will not, be present.

NOTES

1. I use "black" to refer to both black and "Coloured" writers from South Africa, in an attempt to avoid perpetuating the use of the term "Coloured." I will have to use the term, however, where there is an historical necessity to distinguish between the black and Coloured communities under apartheid.

2. Mphahlele, Ezekiel, ". . . Away into Ancestral Fields?", 12. I refer to Bishop here because he provides an excellent summary of the debate between South African and other African writers over negritude. His book, *African Literature, African Critics* is also more easily accessible than many of his sources.

Chapter 5

Women Writers at Home and in Exile: The Examples of Bessie Head and Miriam Tlali

"Home" and "exile": the two terms seem immediately to convey opposite emotional territories, one of comfort and security, the other a place of loneliness and isolation. Yet, for women, and especially women writers, the emotional charge of the home country and the country of exile might be different. Virginia Woolf, in her essay *Three Guineas* makes the famous claim that "as woman, I have no country. As a woman I want no country" (Woolf 109). Since women have not been participants in defining national boundaries and national affairs, Woolf's claim suggests that they "cannot legitimately lay claim either to a national territory or to their own national mythology and history" (Boehmer 5). For Miriam Tlali and Bessie Head, their racial positions in South Africa, as well as their status as women, increase the distance between themselves and the Republic of South Africa. Tlali has remained in South Africa, a voice for black liberation and the creation of a new state, while Head experienced the trauma and the transition of exile, becoming a Botswanian citizen in 1979.

Several recent studies focus on women writers in exile, from *Women's Writing in Exile* (Broe and Ingram, eds.) to *Motherlands: Black Women's Writing from Africa, the Caribbean and South Asia* (Nasta, ed.). Exile may be experienced as homelessness and isolation, or alternatively it can be an experience of great freedom, an opening of possibilities not available in the mother country. Women might find it easier to violate conventions of behavior in a foreign environment, as Susan Stanford Friedman says of the American poet H.D.: "Being expatriate was a spatial metaphor, a geographic manifestation of a more fundamental exile from convention—all kinds of convention" (Friedman 92). Exile can be an opportunity to create a new space for women's writing.

In South Africa, the geographic displacement of black writers, both men and women, has been a forced dislocation, the result of deliberate government policies to try to silence anti-apartheid writers. Bessie Head left South Africa for Botswana with only an exit permit, which did not allow her to return. Head's exile thus differed substantially from the voluntary exile of writers such as H.D. and Ernest Hemingway. Her novels and short stories explore the spaces allotted to the immigrant and to ethnic minorities in Botswana. Questions of alienation and relationship to the land that are central to the works of South African white writers are reworked in the context of the black South African emigrant: what relationship can she establish to the rest of Africa? In her work, Head creates characters who are not just exiles but also immigrants seeking to assimilate into their adoptive country. As Valerie Kibera argues, "Botswana is the country where the protagonists of her novels, like Head herself, sought—and found—a chance for new beginnings, community and a place to call home" (Kibera 320). In her letters, autobiographical essays, and fiction, Head explores this territory, establishing the broad horizon of Africa as the boundary of her life and work.

In contrast to Bessie Head, Miriam Tlali has remained in South Africa, and is one of a very small number of black women writers in that country. When asked in an interview why there are so few black women novelists, Tlali responded: "It [the novel] needs a long time and you have to think about it. And you have to dream about it and black women do not have time to dream" (Lockett 71). Writing from within South Africa, Tlali focuses on the experiences of black women as they negotiate the boundaries and restrictions placed upon them by race, class, and gender. Her first novel, *Muriel at Metropolitan*, is unique among literature by South African women in its restriction of the horizons of the novel to the spatial boundaries of the office where Muriel works. In all of her work, Tlali uses a deliberately limited landscape, emphasizing the restrictions of the physical environment for black South Africans. By placing the landscapes of Bessie Head and Miriam Tlali's fiction side by side, I will reveal the contrasts between them, and yet also see beneath these contrasts their shared concern to expose the boundaries of black women's lives in Southern Africa.

MIRIAM TLALI

Tlali's first novel was *Muriel at Metropolitan*, published in 1979. Since then, she has published another novel, *Amandla*, and two collections of short stories and nonfiction. In *Muriel at Metropolitan*, the landscape of the novel is almost exclusively the main office of Metropolitan Radio, where Muriel works. Metropolitan Radio sells not only radios but also furniture, symbols of status for both the black and lower-class white communities. The office is a "grey area," or rather an overlapping black/white space, which Afrikaner, British, Coloured, Jewish, and black South African workers uncomfortably share. The ethnically mixed community is the creation of the owner, Mr. Bloch, who tries to use his labor pool as economically as possible, meaning in practice that he has hired only three or four white workers, relying on black mechanics, drivers, and sales help to service black customers.

Muriel's arrival in the office creates a disturbance, as the office space had previously been the province of white women workers. They try to partition her off from the white workers: "A more or less convenient place was created for me just below the stairs. I was separated from the rest of the white staff by the cabinets and steel mesh wires" (*Muriel* 15). Even this separation can't be maintained, as Muriel starts to do more of the same work as the white women, and moves back and forth between her desk under the stairs and one in the "white section." Tlali's novel examines the effects of this environment on the workers at Metropolitan Radio.

The white women workers are uncomfortable with the growing equality of space accorded to Muriel: "The crux of the matter was that the white workers did not want to acknowledge their commonness with their black colleagues. As long as the system granted them certain privileges that the other racial groups did not enjoy, then they were contented" (*Muriel* 163). The pressure of business economics within the office makes a shared space for Mrs. Kuhn, Mrs. Stein, and Muriel the most practical solution, but the white women keep trying to preserve some kind of color line within that space.

The black workers are also frustrated within this environment. Expected to be grateful for any signs of better than average treatment, the black workers gradually lose their patience with their white employer, and move on (all except Adam, the first black employee of the firm). Asked to make tea for the other workers, Muriel thinks, "In the Republic of South Africa, the colour of your skin alone condemns you to a position of eternal servitude from which you can never escape" (*Muriel* 117). She will always be less than equal to her fellow workers, no matter how many small victories she has gained.

What finally makes Muriel leave Metropolitan, however, is not her treatment within the office, but her growing realization of how the hire-purchase firm is exploiting its black customers. The insolent second class treatment of the Africans is compounded by the exorbitant interest rates charged to them, and Muriel becomes disgusted with her role in exploiting other blacks: "All I knew was that I could not continue to be part of the web that has been woven to entangle a people whom I love and am part of" (*Muriel* 190). The larger setting, the position of the company in relation to the structure of apartheid in South Africa, is the context of Muriel's decision to quit the firm.

Tlali brilliantly uses her microscopic examination of a mixed workplace to expose the contradictions and complexities of South Africa's apartheid system. Mr. Bloch, a Jewish employer, is an outsider himself in some ways, and he tries to create a viable office environment for his staff, bending and ignoring some of the stricter codes of racial separation. Within this space, however, both black and white workers are frustrated, as it neither provides blacks with true equality (their pay, and their toilet facilities, are always unequal) nor reassures the whites that their putative racial superiority will be respected. Tlali also shows that, while Bloch's business economics within the office may lead to a loosening of strict apartheid regulations, his company's business as a whole is dependent on the apartheid system—most of his money is made on large interest payments on inferior merchandise, paid monthly by black South Africans. Thus Muriel at the end of the novel clearly sees how her "better" working conditions within the office were based on the exploitation of others outside it.

Muriel at Metropolitan is remarkable because of its focus on the workplace. Only once is Muriel seen at home, although she provides glimpses of her domestic activities, such as staying home when her child has smallpox. Tlali has said that the experiences recorded in *Muriel* are autobiographical. She deliberately avoided any description of her home life at that time: "I was a young woman, and I was going to have an ideal home, an ideal life, that kind of thing. . . . But it wasn't to be that way" (Lockett 82). Her protectiveness of her home life led her to leave it out of the novel entirely. This strategy produced a novel in which a black woman is seen, not as a mother (although Muriel is a mother and a wife) but as a worker. In the novel, Muriel's entry into the workplace creates a disturbance; there have been white women and black men working there, but no black women. One of the running themes of the novel is the contention over which toilet Muriel should be allowed to use. This symbolizes the negotiation over defining her place within the social sphere of the office—is she black, or female? While Muriel herself initially uses the women's toilet, the white women object so strenuously that she is forced to use the (black) men's toilet, until another one can be fixed up just for her. Thus Muriel is forced to align herself with her fellow workers by race, not gender.

Tlali has been criticized for subordinating black women to men in her fiction. Dorothy Driver has said, "A writer like Miriam Tlali tends to bolster the image of masculinity, and to reiterate the need for women to stay at home minding the babies and tending the garden while men go out to fight for change" (Driver 238). She points to an early episode in *Muriel at Metropolitan* in which Muriel refuses to ask a black man to run an errand for her: "How could I? He was a man, and I was a woman. According to our custom a woman does not send a man" (*Muriel* 27). This scene with the tea-boy, Johannes, takes place early in the novel. Later in the novel, Muriel is much more aware of her status as an office worker, and offers her resignation when she is asked to make tea for the whites, which is Johannes' usual job. She feels that her status at the workplace has been threatened: "they had gone too far and were treating me with contempt. That soon he would be asking me to wash the floor like Johannes or to go and help carry the stoves" (120). Here, Muriel is no longer advocating black codes of behavior between men and women, but asserting her right to be treated like the white women, who do not make their own tea. Interestingly, Tlali resolves this crisis by the spontaneous act of Mrs. Kuhn, one of Muriel's white coworkers. Avoiding the difficulties presented by asking Muriel to make tea, Mrs. Kuhn orders tea from a shop for herself and for Muriel. Treated like an equal, Muriel's anger subsides. While Tlali is able to avoid showing Johannes bringing Muriel her tea (the role reversal Muriel objected to early in the novel) through the depiction of Mrs. Kuhn's action, there is still a small reminder that this is, in fact,

Johannes' job: "This was to be the procedure in future whenever Johannes was not in the shop at tea-time" (121). Preserving her status as an office worker becomes more important to Muriel than preserving a deferential attitude towards Johannes.

In the only scene set in her home, Muriel praises her husband's attitude towards her: "To him I was someone special in spite of being black. He spoke as if he had a goddess for a wife, not a mere black nanny" (*Muriel* 118). She allows him to compose her resignation letter, and she copies it out in her own handwriting. In this scene, Muriel seems to be meek and subservient, following her husband's decision about what she should do. This resignation is not accepted; Muriel continues to work in the office, and now she is also brought tea, like the white women. She has used the resignation letter to improve her situation. When, at the end of the novel, she writes her own letter of resignation, she thinks, "I remembered the resignation note I had once written, after so many false starts, wavering, uncertain, and compared it to that final one. My handwriting had never looked so beautiful" (190). While Muriel does not challenge her husband's authority directly, Tlali shows her actions to be effective only when they are the result of her own decision, not his. Now the letter is delivered, and Muriel is free to leave.

As Muriel becomes more disgusted with her role in exploiting blacks economically, she becomes more overt in challenging her white coworkers' vision of the South African nation. Mrs. Stein says, "South Africa is a most peaceful country. People are free to go where they like, and say what they feel" (*Muriel* 177). Muriel responds by pointing out that blacks are completely restricted in where they can live and how they move about the country, because of the pass laws. Muriel and Mrs. Stein also disagree about the role of the Bantustans, as Muriel reminds them that the so-called citizens of the Transkei are mostly black workers in South Africa, who have never seen the Transkei. Muriel comments, "They seemed amazed. It was as if I was saying things they had never heard before" (179). Finally, Mrs. Stein raises the argument that "the Bantus here are better off than those in the other African countries" (179). This is Mrs. Stein's vision of the world: a peaceful white South Africa surrounded by black Bantustans and poor, mismanaged African nations. Muriel counters her vision by denying the validity, even the reality, of the Bantustans as independent homelands, and draws her attention to the inequalities within South Africa when she asks if either of her coworkers would be willing to exchange places with her.

Muriel is aware of the larger landscape of Southern Africa; there are references to Zambia, and to terrorist groups in Angola and Mozambique. Muriel's own mother lives in Lesotho, and hopes that her daughter will come to her there:

She could not see that the destiny of the one million Basotho would always be intermingled with that of the teeming millions of voiceless, helpless races surrounding them, that no protective moat could ever be built round Lesotho. . . . All she wanted to do was to redeem her own; to grab me to safety before I too, sank in the quicksand with all the others. The Republic was beyond redemption. (*Muriel* 139)

As in her argument with her white coworkers, Muriel denies that the Bantustans, or Lesotho and Swaziland, represent a solution to the problems she faces in South Africa. She doesn't want an individual solution that simply saves herself, but liberation for all of her people. In this way, while the setting of the novel is within the limits of the office spaces at Metropolitan Radio, Miriam Tlali situates her heroine's predicament within the struggle for freedom of all black people in South Africa.

In *Amandla*, Tlali uses a different strategy. The novel has a larger scope, representing life in Soweto and surrounding areas during the Soweto uprisings of 1976-77. Tlali has constructed the novel out of the voices of her characters; most of the work is dialogue, discussions of events, policies, political positions, and family issues. *Amandla* represents the voices of Soweto, including parents, children, policemen, revolutionaries, students, and teachers. Within this oral framework, only a few locations are specifically described, heightening their importance: Gramsy's matchbox house, which is also the home of her grandson Pholoso, a student leader; Rockville Lake in Soweto; funeral scenes; street scenes; an underground room, and a prison cell. These settings firmly anchor the novel in the physical environment of Soweto.

Gramsy's house serves as a center for her extended family; it is also a place of refuge for her grandchildren, and occasionally for her battered niece as well. Visitors constantly drop in, bringing news and discussing current events. As Pholoso's home, Gramsy's house also serves as a symbol of the environment from which the student movement grew. Gramsy's dignity and determination are reflected in Pholoso's actions as a student leader. The home she has maintained to ensure the physical survival of her grandchildren shows both the accomplishments and the limitations of previous generations. Gramsy has been able to provide for the physical well-being of her children and grandchildren, but she only rents her house, and cannot own it; their security is precarious. The students' demands for an end to apartheid, and especially to the Group Areas Act and unequal education, are more radical than previous efforts, and more organized. Tlali shows how the students' work is not necessarily in opposition to previous attempts to gain limited freedoms, but a natural extension of those efforts. Through Gramsy's complicity in her grandson's work, Tlali shows how a black South African family's intergenerational network supports the students, providing food, clothing, and temporary shelter for the fugitives.

The street and funeral scenes provide a larger, political landscape, showing the decrepitude of Soweto and the courage of the black students defying white military power: "The mourners joined in the singing, joining the school-children as they marched past the long columns of waiting police-vans—anxious, gleaming eyes just visible through the heavily-wired windows" (*Amandla* 75). The secret underground room where Pholoso lectures other students on revolutionary tactics, and the prison cell where he is incarcerated, form a stark background for Pholoso's activities. Both places are spartan, unadorned cells created by the pressures of the white regime.

Rockville Lake is a more complex symbol; weedy, choked with debris, and malodorous, it is obviously one more example of the decayed environment of Soweto, and yet there is also movement and hope in this landscape. The lake is connected by a river to other townships, suggesting the possibility of unified action: "The river meanders on, digging dongas right across the locations of Phiri, Mapetla, Senoane and Moroka, where it broadens out to form the Moroka Lake, and flows on through Klipspruit, Orlando and Mzimhlope to an 'unknown' destination" (*Amandla* 62). Significantly, it is the location Tlali chooses for the closing scene of her novel.

Pholoso must flee into Swaziland; his girlfriend, Felleng, will remain behind in Soweto. Tlali isolates these figures in the veld surrounding Rockville Lake: "The deserted streets and the bare veld between Moroka and Dlamini Townships through which they had been moving provided an agreeable background to their desire to be alone with each other" (*Amandla* 291). Pholoso moves off into the dawn: "[Felleng] looked at the receding figure until it was a mere dot against the horizon, where the twilight of a new day was already becoming visible, and she turned to go" (294). This conclusion to the novel is melodramatic, yet it also is consistent with Tlali's presentation of the novel as an oral history of the Soweto uprising. The "new day" of Felleng's thought is borrowed from the rhetoric of the Soweto uprising itself.

Tlali's more recent work, *Mihloti*, is a collection of journalism, interviews, and a short story. In this work, Tlali reveals the range of her use of landscape techniques, from factual reportage to highly symbolic treatments of the landscape of South Africa. In her first piece, she describes being arrested and detained in a prison cell. Here, she uses a spare, reportorial style that works well since there is no need to embellish the details, as the facts are horrifying enough. In "Setsumi's Qoqolosi," on the other hand, she explores the meaning of this peak for herself, comparing it to Mount Everest, and also contrasting it to her everyday life in Soweto. She imagines the life of a woman in Lesotho: "You sweep his mother's *lelapa,* and with every stroke you make, in your heart you hum a love tune in memory of your lover while you cast a longing look at the Qoqolosi—pillar of your strength—enshrouded in the early morning mist giving its typical, haunting, mysterious look" (*Mihloti* 67-68). The lovers' relationship is both contained in and symbolized by the landscape. Tlali admits the fantastic character of this image: "Some dreams you have to abandon as unattainable" (*Mihloti* 68). The purpose of the dream, however, is to recapture an image of human life as it could be lived by blacks in South Africa, versus the realities of Soweto: "There, she would very likely be standing in a dark alley between huge blocks of flats, trying to derive some pleasure out of a few stolen moments amid throngs of milling passers-by" (67).

In the same story, Tlali points to the investiture of names with meaning, beginning with the devaluing of "Bethlehem" from a Scriptural mystery to an apartheid rail station in South Africa which shares that name: "*Betleleme . . .* Even the very way the Basotho pronounce the word with the tongue sticking out and the lips twisted down at both ends suggested repulsion" (*Mihloti* 58). Qoqolosi is both Setsumi's Qoqolosi, connected to a revered Basotho leader, and the backdrop for Thomas Mofolo's Pitseng valley—it is a place with a specific history, as well as personal significance for Tlali. These layers of significance create the powerful sense of place experienced by Tlali at the peak of the mountain. She ends the piece hoping that future generations will protect the Qoqolosi as a national monument—a Basotho national monument.

A final image from Tlali's work reveals again her ability to represent the complex mix of sentiment and politics, personal and national issues, that permeates black experience in South Africa. Tlali recalls a trip at New Year's to Klipvoor Dam, a small, bedraggled resort for blacks in Bophuthatswana. With her friends, Tlali watches the dawn rise over the water on New Year's Day. This image, with its hopeful implications, is overlaid with another: "The man lowered his head (probably from exhaustion) and sank it into the angle between his forearm and the biceps and remained in that position like a weeping child. . . . To me the whole spectacle suggested the perfect illustration of loneliness" (*Mihloti* 106). Tlali suggests that the man "was very likely trying to escape from the helplessness of a lifetime of unfulfilled aspirations—an existence where hopes and dreams remain forever a receding mirage" (106). The beauty of the South African landscape is a backdrop for the restrictions and frustrations of the lives of black South Africans—clearly represented as unnatural and inhuman conditions. Tlali's restrained use of landscape description intensifies the significance of those locations she does represent: Rockville Lake, Klipvoor Dam and Metropolitan Radio take on archetypal significance as images that mark the boundaries of black South African lives.

BESSIE HEAD

Bessie Head, in contrast to Tlali, wrote most of her fiction in exile. The outlines of her life are well-known: born to a white woman and a black man in South Africa, in 1964 she left for Botswana and the uncertain life of an undocumented person, finally becoming a Botswanian citizen in 1979. The posthumous publication of her letters (*A Gesture of Belonging: Letters from Bessie Head, 1965-1979*) and autobiographical writings (*A Woman Alone*) fill in this outline, and illuminate some of the choices Head made in her fiction. One of the most pressing themes in her fiction is the question of belonging, of community and exile, which is reflected not only in her description of the human characters in her novels, but also in her descriptions of the land itself. Her characters, especially Margaret in *Maru* and Elizabeth in *A Question of Power* struggle with Head's own dilemmas: as a South African "Coloured," what is her position in Botswana? A transient? A refugee? An exile? Or, as she finally became, a Botswanian citizen and writer?

Her letters show that Head experienced Botswana first as a land of exile: "I'm such an isolated goddam outsider trying to be an African of Africa" (*Letters* 24). Head's reference to Botswana as Africa, reveals that she sees South Africa as isolated from the rest of the continent—this new country, Botswana, will be her first experience of real Africa, black Africa. In this new African environment, in the country of the black man, Head was horribly disillusioned by the racialism, tribalism, and corruption she found. Her isolation was overwhelming:

Perhaps I'd be lost anywhere else but it's been Batswana people I've been fighting with, so God help me, and that does not endear me to anyone, especially as I'm some kind of half-caste. You've no idea how frightened I really am because I thought Africa was my home and now I don't know what to do. (*Letters* 37)

Africa should be home for an African, yet, Head, as "some kind of half-caste," discovers that she will not be accepted into Botswana society so easily.

Botswana at this point for Head is a place of drought, of silence, and of a tightly-knit, hostile community: "Little by little I became aware of the most terrible brutality in this quiet-seeming village. Nothing ever happens. There are only people and animals here and starvation, fear, frustration and dog-eat-dog" (*Letters* 9). As Cecil Abrahams has said, "Botswana, the place of escape, becomes the area where there is a 'total de-mystifying of all illusions'" (Abrahams 9).

Early on, however, Head felt the potential of Botswana for herself as a writer: "I believe there are places of fantastic beauty to describe in Africa. I'd just have a whale of a time if I can get me established as a writer of Africa" (*Letters* 25).

Head wants to describe Africa in monumental terms, in contrast to the image she has of the English landscape:

England as a country is very familiar to me as a mental picture. You can't as a writer in Africa go in for such delicate, detailed descriptions of landscape the way English writers used to. The land is too vast and monumental. The power of the carvings of ancient Egyptian civilisation come nearest to an expression of Africa. (*Letters* 70)

In these letters, we can see Head already conceptualizing her residency in Botswana as a residency in Africa. She is experiencing, not a country, but a continent, reaching all the way to Egypt. Her own position then, as an undocumented alien, becomes a challenge to Africa, a call to Pan-Africanism to accept her, to accept the Coloured, the half-castes, and to leave behind tribalism and racialism. Head does not stop here; she conceives of herself as a writer for all races: "Some people can hog the b[l]ack skin for themselves but I have to opt for mankind as a whole" (*Letters* 64). Head herself was rejected by some black nationalists in South Africa as "not black enough" (*Letters* 64). In Botswana, she was similarly rejected as a half-caste. Through her experiences, Head develops a philosophy that rejects all distinctions by color, tribe or appearance: "There is nothing left now but a love which includes others as my own self" (*Letters* 76).

While living in Serowe, Head enrolled in a course on Tropical Agriculture, and, perhaps because of her frustrations with the obstructions and hostility she came into contact with in her human relations, one can hear her relief and even admiration when she considers the life of plants:

Plants are actually a very superior form of life. They are economically viable. They are the only form of life which manufactures its own food . . . I am just studying a thunderous description of this whole process, and it is the self-absorbed habits of plant life which so touch and fascinate my heart. No care about anything, just this inner concentration on creating energy and releasing it. (*Letters* 68-69)

It is not surprising, then, that in her ideal world, plants and humans are in harmony with each other: "It is the oneness of the soul with all living things, whether human or animal or vegetable." She calls it "this unity of the soul with life" (*Letters* 76). Head's vision has only come to her through her suffering: "Most times it is I who take the most blows and learn the deepest lessons" (*Letters* 69).

Given this philosophy (and Head's very practical interest in agriculture), Head's use of landscape in her fiction takes on a deeper significance.

Maru opens on a scene which threatens drought:

The rains were so late that year. But throughout that hot, dry summer those black storm clouds clung in thick folds of brooding darkness along the low horizon . . . each evening they broke the long, sullen silence of the day, and sent soft rumbles of thunder and flickering slicks of lightening across the empty sky. They were not promising rain. They were prisoners, pushed back, in trapped coils of boiling cloud (*Maru* 5).

Rain, or rather the lack of rain, reveals the village's dependence on the natural world, and threatens disaster. Within this environment, however, Maru himself feels at home: "There was so little to disturb his heart within his immediate environment. It was here where he could communicate freely with all the magic and beauty inside him" (*Maru* 7). He is the hereditary ruler of the village, linked by blood and tradition, not just to the village, but to the land itself.

Margaret Cadmore, by contrast, is an outsider, an orphan, daughter of a Masarwa woman, brought up by a white missionary. Margaret, like Head herself, doesn't easily fit into traditional categories: "[She] was hardly African or anything but something new and universal, a type of personality that would be unable to fit into a definition of something as narrow as tribe or race or nation" (*Maru* 16). She has learned "that something was wrong with her relationship to the world" (17) as other children despise and ignore her. Her first vision of the village seems to be a vision of community:

She walked to the door. Below her the village of Dilepe spread out and swept towards the horizon. It was a network of pathways and dusty roads weaving in and out between a tortured lay-out of mud huts. . . . That peace, and those darkening evening shadows were to be the rhythm of her life throughout the year, and Dilepe village was to seem the most beautiful village on earth.

She was really no longer lonely. (*Maru* 31)

Symbolically, the village becomes the horizon of Margaret's experience, eclipsing the missionary school and her previous experiences. The landscape of the village is marked by the human life that is lived within it. It is a "network of pathways" which reveal the connections between specific peoples and spaces through the paths inscribed in the earth. The seeming peacefulness of this vision, however, is disturbed by the reference to the "tortured lay-out of mud huts," suggesting that the twists and turns in the village paths reflect some pain or conflict at the heart of the village, perhaps a foreshadowing of the ethnic conflict between the Batswana and Masarwa people of the village. The narrator's claim that Dilepe village was to "*seem* the most beautiful village on earth" also suggests that the harmony of this image is only temporary. Margaret's vision of the village takes place in the afterglow of her lover Moleka's presence; as Head herself remarks in an interview, "The whole of Dilepe is hallowed ground [for Margaret] because Moleka loves her" (Adler, et al. 19). The landscape is temporarily transformed through Moleka and Margaret's passion.

Much later in the novel, Margaret gazes at the village again, and thinks:

In the distance, a village proceeded with its own life but she knew not what it was—who married, who died, who gave birth to children—nor the reason why two women on her pathway back and forth to school, continually insulted each other in vile language for stealing each other's husbands. She was not a part of it and belonged nowhere. (*Maru* 93)

Like Head herself, Margaret has been disillusioned by the tribalism in her village. The pathways, even her own path from home to school, do not establish connections with the human community of the village. The implication of connection and harmony suggested by the connecting paths is, for Margaret, an illusion of community.

While Margaret is initially drawn to Moleka, Head intends that she will marry Maru. One of the mysterious connections between Margaret and Maru is the way that her paintings are representations of his dreams, as if he has forced her to share his visions. Maru's dreams are of a new world, beyond tribalism. He rejects his inherited post as ruler, and marries Margaret in an effort to lead the village into this future. The village rejects him: "They thought he was dead and would trouble them no more" (*Maru* 126). They do not see any value in his visions, and keep to their traditional ways.

Head's vision of the soul's kingdom is interactive; each figure is not isolated, but draws others into its orbit. In this way, the spiritual landscape is overlaid on the external landscape, transforming the novel. Maru has the potential to make his vision a reality; his marriage to Margaret challenges the village's prejudices. Even though they reject him, this act opens the landscape for other Masarwas: "A door silently opened on the small, dark airless room in which their souls had been shut for a long time. . . . They started to run out into the sunlight, then they turned and looked at the dark, small room. They said: 'We are not going back there'" (*Maru* 126-127). Zoë Wicomb sees this social change as the result of the insertion of Margaret's desires into Maru's dreams: "Head clandestinely represents the heroine's resistance to total subjugation through creating a space in which she could insert inventions of her own, representing her own desires" (Wicomb 43). Thus Margaret, more than Maru, has effected this change—it is her presence in village life that has opened the Masarwa landscape.

Maru begins at the chronological end of the story, with Margaret and Maru living in their house outside the village. This ending undermines Margaret's role as a model for the Masarwa, taking her out of the village completely. Strangely, Maru has lined the path to the house with daisies, as if to imply that Margaret and Maru's relationship will be based on a European romantic pattern, or perhaps to emphasize Head's desire that Maru leave behind traditional ways. In this section of the novel, Margaret is firmly established within the home, yet Maru sees her as still divided in her affections between himself and Moleka: "There were two rooms. In one his wife totally loved him; in the other, she totally loved Moleka" (*Maru* 8). Ultimately, Maru cannot control all of Margaret's emotions. The use of the metaphor of the two rooms suggests that Margaret herself moves freely between them, while Maru is shut out of the space devoted to Moleka. In addition, the representation of her "two-roomed" soul suggests a lack of resolution; even though she is now alone with Maru, Margaret continues to desire Moleka as well, a desire the novel cannot fulfill. Margaret's desire stubbornly refuses to be confined to the monogamous space of marriage.

In *A Question of Power*, Head introduces Elizabeth, a character whose biography closely mirrors her own—born to a white woman in a mental hospital in South Africa, kept from the knowledge of her own heritage until age thirteen, she marries and then leaves for Botswana to become a teacher. After this, however, the story becomes the story of Elizabeth's insanity, and the landscape for a time is reduced to the walls of her own home, as she holds long conversations with Sello's spirit. Sello discusses Hinduism, Buddha, Egyptian gods, reincarnation—a host of what would now be called "New Age" ideas. Elizabeth wonders—is she insane? Is this a religious vision?

The landscape of *A Question of Power* is more clearly defined than that of *Maru*. Motabeng is a Botswanian village: "It took a stranger some time to fall in love with its harsh outlines and stark, black trees" (*Question* 19-20). The bush surrounds the village:

The bush began just at the edge of Motabeng and contrasted vividly in beauty with the starkness of central village with its endless circles of mud huts. The bush was a wild, expansive landscape dotted with wind-bent, umbrella-shaped thorn trees. . . . Motabeng Secondary School had been built right amidst this wilderness of solitude and slumber. (*Question* 55)

Elizabeth calls Motabeng "Village of the Rain Wind" which identifies it with Serowe where Head herself lived. Elizabeth has an appreciation for the rhythms and values of traditional farming; she stares wistfully after the women heading to the fields. The human and natural worlds overlap each other: "There was no sharp distinction between the circling mud walls of a hut and the earth outside" (*Question* 60). "Tholo's pumpkin" becomes a symbol to Elizabeth of a complicated interrelationship between life and work, spirit and nature. She leaves teaching and works in an experimental garden, trying to encourage the villagers to use techniques developed at the school under a black South African principal and at projects under the guidance of Europeans. Head explicitly praises foreign development projects: "It always helped, too, when people from other lands took note of the future greatness of the African continent" (72). Head also reveals her joy in the African landscape:

The dawn came. The soft shifts and changes of light stirred with a slow wonder over the vast expanse of the African sky. A small bird in a tree outside awoke and trilled loudly. The soft, cool air, so fresh and full of the perfume of the bush, swirled around her face and form as she stood watching the sun thrust one powerful, majestic, golden arm above the horizon. (*Question* 100)

Here, Head integrates Elizabeth with her environment, describing how the light, like Elizabeth, "stirred with a slow wonder." The air swirls around her, and her gaze then draws attention back to the sun, which she is watching.

Kenosi and the American, Tom, help Elizabeth with her garden. They work to bring in water, to plant in rotation, and mulch the rows of vegetables. Other volunteers join them. Scenes with these characters alternate with hallucinatory visions, frightening Elizabeth with the possibility of another nervous breakdown. Elizabeth herself comes to be called the "Cape Gooseberry" because of her efforts at growing and promoting that fruit: "The work had a melody like that—a complete stranger like the Cape Gooseberry settled down and became part of the village life of Motabeng" (*Question* 153). This comparison is telling—the sturdy, foreign bush takes root and produces abundantly in its new environment. Through this image, Head shows the productiveness of immigration, hybrids, and exotics, both in the human and natural worlds—an image of an increase of energy through the process of migration. Recently, in an interview with Bill Moyer, the American writer Bharati Mukherjee said much the same thing—that immigration should be seen not as a loss, not as homelessness and exile, but as gain, for both the immigrant and the new country. And yet, Elizabeth is still battling in her mind with the spirit of Dan, who insists: "She was not genuinely African; *he* had to give her the real African insight" (*Question* 159). It takes another breakdown and a final conversation with Sello before she can feel that she has put Dan behind her.

Elaine Savory Fido, in writing about Head and other women exiles, claims, "Exile, then, becomes a space in which hurt can be explored and contained within the creation of fictions" (Fido 346). In both *Maru* and *A Question of Power*, Head explores the psychic space of mixed race parentage and the pressures and prejudices experienced by those who are not black or white in the deeply divided society of South Africa. But exile, for Head, is also figured as a kind of homecoming, as the ending of the novel suggests: "As she fell asleep, she placed one soft hand over her land. It was a gesture of belonging" (*Question* 206). It is a powerful and poignant moment, showing the immigrant's desire for community, and finally, her ability to succeed. The garden, neglected while she was in the hospital, will be replanted. The community will forgive her for her excesses, and is willing to include her again.

In this novel, then, Head interweaves land and community. The connection is more clearly worked out than in *Maru*. Maru wants to plant daisies as a symbol of his love. In *A Question of Power*, Elizabeth grows food for the village, improving their lives. The connection is tangible rather than symbolic. Even more, the garden of exotics, hybrids, and experiments thriving in Botswana replicates the community of refugees from South Africa, volunteers from Europe, and local Botswanians who form a community through their joint efforts in *A Question of Power*. As Kibera asserts, "The co-operative is Head's antidote to the exclusions of tribe, race, class and gender that operate in Southern Africa" (Kibera 326). The outsider can become a thriving member of the whole.

In her own life, and in the lives of her characters, belonging and connection only come through suffering. Bessie Head's Serowe, the Village of the Rain Wind, is an image of the future, of the bricolage of immigrants and natives, of the creation as well as preservation of culture. It is a map of the postcolonial predicament located within the larger space of African history. The landscape of exile has become a map of the world: "I am the ocean in which all things live and move and have their being and for them to think they are separate and apart from my life is not possible" (*Letters* 76). Through her descriptions of cooperative efforts, of people rising above racial and tribal prejudices, Head tries to coax such a world into being. She also places herself, not only within the immediate community, but also within the world, suggesting that all life is connected. In commenting on the perspective she uses in her novels, Head claims, "The cool stance means: you are up on a horizon, you have the biggest view possible" (Adler 12-13).

Head's work reveals the place of exile. Her Botswana is a place of community and isolation, pleasures and pain; her characters demand to be let into a society that is not readily open to outsiders. Assimilation requires greatness, effort, and desire on both sides, and it is never a complete assimilation but rather, in her own image, a cooperative garden. The landscape of Botswana, despite its bleakness and its droughts, is a landscape full of potential.

Miriam Tlali, in her work, takes a very different approach. Rather than depicting the potential for a future, more harmonious society, she concentrates on exposing the landscape of contemporary South Africa:

I don't think I should at this time in our history be involved in a lot of talking and dreaming about the beautiful skies and the moon, and so on, and dreaming about ideal situations when we don't have them. In the very first place I wouldn't have taken to writing, I wouldn't stick to it when it is so difficult. Except for the fact that I see in it some kind of exposure: it gives me the opportunity to expose what we feel inside. (Lockett 76-77)

Here the pressures of "this time in history" are very clear, preventing her, perhaps, from exploring the full range of her imaginative powers. Yet at the same time this focus gives a special clarity and sharpness to Tlali's use of detail in her landscapes, as each scene resonates with the injustice and inhumanity of the social and economic system in South Africa.

Each of these writers, then, imbues the landscape with social significance. Head forges a vision of a new society, cooperative, unprejudiced, and in harmony with the landscape, producing gardens in the desert. Tlali's varied landscapes all trace the social configurations that constrain and control relationships to the land and to the nation. Clearly the landscape of Soweto in *Amandla* reveals the necessity of liberation in South Africa. In both writers' work, the home country is one which must be fought for and realized through struggle; "exile" might be only a stage on the way towards home. Thus these African women writers transform the traditional language of home and exile to create a space for their own predicaments and desires, redrawing the boundaries of their lives.

Chapter 6

"And Then the Bush Avenged Itself": The Landscape of White South African Fiction

And then the bush avenged itself: that was her last thought.
—Doris Lessing, *The Grass Is Singing* 243

For white South African writers, the landscape of South Africa is scored with the history of an oppression which seems to preclude any natural relationship to the land. In the novels of André Brink, Nadine Gordimer, and J.M. Coetzee, white characters have a difficult time feeling at home in the landscape. Sentiments like Mary Turner's in Lessing's novel, that the bush itself resents her presence, are common. If they reject the idea that white conquest and domination have created a right to ownership in South Africa (as all three writers have), what other relationship to the land can they establish for their white characters? On what basis can they claim to be African? In a review written in 1958, Doris Lessing claims that "all white African literature is the literature of exile: not from Europe, but from Africa" (Lessing, "Desert Child" 700). André Brink's *A Dry White Season*, Nadine Gordimer's *July's People* and J.M. Coetzee's *Waiting for the Barbarians* can all be read as novels of exile.

Since the beginnings of white settlement, the landscape of South Africa has been fragmented into a shifting patchwork of Boer republics, British colonies, and "tribal homelands." This pattern has continued into the present; the Afrikaners and the descendants of the British own most of the land, while Africans live in locations, townships, servants' quarters, miners' dormitories, or in the former homelands created by the South African government. Only a few have made the transition to new houses in formerly all-white neighborhoods. In each of the novels in this chapter, white characters find themselves seeing parts of the country with which they are completely unfamiliar, yet which have always been present alongside their own white areas. Their homes and communities come to seem constricted, fragile, and illusory, dependent on the black locations around them while simultaneously trying to deny the importance, even the existence of black spaces within South Africa. Each character comes to realize Hegel's claim that the masters are dependent on the slaves. The future looks even more bleak: without a legitimate relationship to the land, what right do whites have to stay on in Africa? As Nadine Gordimer says in her 1959 essay, "Where Do Whites Fit In?": "if we're going to fit in at all in the new Africa, it's going to be sideways, where-we-can, wherever-they'll-shift-up-for-us. This will not be comfortable" ("Whites" 32). The white South African would "do well to regard himself as an immigrant to a new country; somewhere he has never lived before, but to whose life he has committed himself" ("Whites" 34). In each of the novels discussed in this chapter, characters seek a place for themselves in Africa.

ANDRÉ BRINK

André Brink's *A Dry White Season* is narrated by a writer of sentimental novels. He has been mailed a bundle of documents by Ben Du Toit, an Afrikaner school teacher who was hit by a car and killed a few days later. The novel moves between a first person voice based on Ben's journals and on the novelist's imaginative reconstruction of his thoughts and feelings, and a more objective third person voice in which the narrator records what happens to Ben. As in eighteenth century novels, the use of a frame tale, and of a narrator/editor lend an air of authenticity to the narrative; in addition, first Ben's actions and then the novelist's provide models of response for the reader, as both characters try to decide what to do with the information they receive.

In the novel, Ben discovers that the Special Branch has been covering up the details of the disappearances of Jonathan Ngubene and his father, Gordon. Ben knows these people, and he becomes involved in trying to discover the truth about what happened to them in detention. In this investigation, he is forced to recognize the dark underside of his society, the brutality and oppression which enforce Afrikaner values. He himself becomes the object of the Special Branch's attention, and he gradually loses his family, his job, and his friends as he insists on continuing his investigation. After Ben Du Toit dies, the novelist decides to write the story so that "it will not be possible for any man ever to say again: *I knew nothing about it*" (*White Season* 316, Brink's italics).

Ben Du Toit is a history teacher. Earlier, Ben believed in the Afrikaners' version of history, which characterized them as the first freedom fighters of Africa, but he rapidly becomes disillusioned. As he appeals to the authorities, and to the dominee of his church, in his search for truth, he is met by the protective wall of the "laager," the circle of wagons used during the Great Trek to protect the Boers from attack. It is better, they tell him, not to know, not to ask, but to trust them. When Ben hears schoolchildren singing the South African national anthem, "*at thy will to live or perish, O South Africa, our land!*" (*White Season* 160, Brink's italics), it takes on a sinister meaning: he thinks of the murders in the name of national security of South Africans by the Special Branch.

Ben Du Toit's life is lived in enclosed spaces. He has his study, his home, the school where he teaches, and the church he attends on Sundays. His life is orderly and precise, following his own habitual patterns. He closely associates other people's lives with their environments, particularly with the rooms in their houses. His son's room is "A wilderness in which he felt an imposter" (*White Season* 81). Emily Ngubene's house in Soweto is "cement and corrugated iron. . . . Inside, a spattering of old calendars and religious pictures on the bare walls; no ceiling to hide the iron roof above; dining table and chairs; a couple of gas lamps; sewing machine; transistor radio" (92). These passages imply a strong connection between people's lives and their possessions. Mrs. Ngubene's home exposes her poverty, but also her industry. Ben's identity is closely associated with his own home; he walks through the rooms "as if he were walking through himself, through the rooms of his mind and the passages and hollows of his own arteries and glands and viscera" (81). As he begins to learn about the activities of the Special Branch, he becomes unable to relate himself to these rooms: "He felt like a visitor from a distant land arriving in a city where all the inhabitants had been overcome by the plague. . . . He was alone in an incomprehensible expanse" (81). He is alienated from his home, and from the patterns of his life which the rooms imply.

In this phase, when Ben Du Toit is in one location, the other locations he knows seem unreal to him. Entering Soweto, he feels "a sensation of total strangeness as they reached the first rows of identical brick buildings. Not just another city, but another country, another dimension, a wholly different world" (*White Season* 89). Ben has never been to Soweto before, even though he has lived in Johannesburg for years. He is appalled at the conditions in the townships, things that he has heard about, but hasn't fully appreciated: "It was—well, like the dark side of the moon" (96). His sense of the difference of life in Soweto makes him, on returning to his home, see it as alien:

And all at once *this* was what seemed foreign to him: not what he'd seen in the course of the long bewildering afternoon, but this. His garden, with the sprinkler on the lawn. His house, with white walls, and orange tiled roof, and windows, and rounded stoep. His wife appearing in the front door. As if he'd never seen it before in his life (*White Season* 99).

Throughout the story, Ben has difficulty seeing these different places as being on the same plane of reality; they are in different worlds. The most ominous world is that of the Security Branch, in John Vorster Square. Ben remembers the gate "which is carefully locked behind you, effectively severing all links with the world outside" (58). Ben sees how the police, and Afrikaner society in general, work to create and maintain the boundaries between worlds, preventing people from feeling any connection with those who live somewhere else. They invade his world, however, and destroy his boundaries, as he tries to confront them. They open his mail, tap his phone, enlist even his daughter as an informer. While the police maintain their own boundaries, they are frighteningly efficient at breaking down the barriers seemingly protecting Ben's privacy.

The novel presents human life as fundamentally isolated. Even when Ben goes into the mountains with Melanie and her father, a philosophy professor, Ben cannot assume that they share his experience of this environment. Ben fantasizes about building a house on the mountain and living there with Melanie, away from all of the enclosures and difficulties of his life in Johannesburg. Melanie's father immediately breaks the illusion, insisting that Ben cannot, even in imagination, escape from his responsibility to protest against injustice in South Africa. Ben's inability is not personal, but political—he cannot turn his back on the problems of his society.

While Ben has to reject the veld and return to the city, his metaphors for his situation increasingly use an image of the desert. The title of the novel originally applies to a drought that occurred in Ben's childhood. He and his father had to kill their own sheep one by one, as the water supply dried up and the animals couldn't survive. Increasingly, Ben sees his current position as similar to this bleak episode in his past. Even the searing memory of the drought, however, becomes less painful than his current uncertainty and paranoia: "If only it had been a real desert in which one could die of thirst or exposure. . . . For then, at least, one would know what was happening" (*White Season* 285). The metaphor of the drought is inadequate for expressing Du Toit's disorientation and the pressures of his current life; this "dry season" in society is worse than what the land can inflict on him.

In *A Dry White Season*, Brink uses metaphors of enclosure and the desert landscape to show the isolation of the anti-apartheid Afrikaner in South Africa. In Brink's essays on the position of the Afrikaner writer, he uses similar language, referring to maps, territories and geographies of literature in his collection *Writing in a State of Siege*. In this collection, he examines the "place" of literature in South Africa, and also the place of the Afrikaner writer. Through this examination, he places his own literary productions within the political context of his embattled country.

Fiction, for Brink, is a map of the world:

The writer is not concerned only with 'reproducing' the real. What he does is to perceive, below the lines of the map he draws, the contours of another world, somehow a more 'essential' world. And from the interaction between the land as he *perceives* it to be and the land as he knows it *can* be, someone from outside, the 'reader' of the map, watches—and aids—the emergence of the *meaning* of the map. (*Writing in a State of Siege* 169)

Through his cartographical metaphor, Brink neatly balances the position of literature between the imaginary and the real: the map is a fiction, but it is a fiction intimately connected with the real. This is the role of literature: "what is offered by literature functioning as myth in a bewildering and secular age, is to *imagine the real.* Not to avoid what *is*, by offering a substitute or a palliative, but to experience what exists so intensely that through the imagination it realizes its full potential" (*Writing in a State of Siege* 221, Brink's italics). Defining literature in this way, Brink sees writing as an integral part of political action and commitment in South Africa, pointing to the government's use of banning and censorship as signs that they, too, see the significance of writing as a political act. In *A Dry White Season*, writing is also a political act; Ben Du Toit mails his writings to the unnamed novelist, who creates the narrative that the reader reads. The security forces have been trying to confiscate Ben's papers; by rewriting them and publishing them, the narrator risks Ben's fate. Through this structure, Brink emphasizes the act of writing, and the political risk of writing; both Ben and the narrator are aware of the possible consequences of their actions. The narrator also models a reader's response. He not only publishes Ben's notes, but creates a new text that builds on the notes. It is a text for which he must take responsibility. The reader then, is challenged to author a text—an action, a response—to the novel; it is not enough, it is implied, to read it. Brink links his text to the world through this multiple authorship/readership. The fact that *A Dry White Season* was banned in South Africa adds another layer of political meaning to the text.

Brink won the Martin Luther King Memorial Prize for *A Dry White Season*. In his acceptance speech, he said, "In *A Dry White Season* I have tried to accept that responsibility one owes to one's society and one's time; it was conceived in anguish and written in pain and in rage, but not in hate" (*Writing in a State of Siege* 204). Brink wrote the novel first in Afrikaans, and then rewrote it in English. In English, it is part of a body of anti-apartheid literature, including works by Gordimer, Coetzee, Fugard and others. In Afrikaans, it has a different role. While challenging the Afrikaner community to accept that one of their own is against apartheid, it also attempts to rescue the language of Afrikaans from being condemned as the language of apartheid. Along with the other *Sestiger* writers, Brink uses Afrikaans in order to save it. The Afrikaans language was the immediate cause of the Soweto uprisings in 1976, when the South African government tried to enforce the use of Afrikaans as the only language of instruction in schools. For black South Africans, it was the language of a despised authority: the government, the police, the prison guards. Other than the Afrikaners themselves, only a small population of "Cape Coloureds" has Afrikaans as its mother tongue. In this context, Brink's use of both Afrikaans and English for his writing is a way to overcome the international isolation of the Afrikaner community, without abandoning his mother tongue entirely. *A Dry White Season* claims a space for itself within both Afrikaans and English, challenging the boundaries between these two linguistic communities while it also challenges the physical and psychological boundaries between races created by apartheid.

NADINE GORDIMER

Nadine Gordimer is probably the best known South African writer outside of South Africa. Unlike Brink, she has had a large international audience for her work, but like him, she has seen several of her novels banned in South Africa. Indeed, in the international community, the banning of a novel in South Africa may be its badge of honor. By choosing Gordimer in 1991, the Pulitzer committee seemed to be tacitly acknowledging the importance of Gordimer's anti-apartheid stance, and honoring her part in agitating for change in South Africa.

In her own essays, however, Gordimer has acknowledged that her own position is not so easy to define. As a white in South Africa, she inevitably participates in, and benefits from apartheid. She is privileged in her education, economic opportunities, freedom to travel, and in her access to the international literary scene. While in *The Essential Gesture* Gordimer develops an analysis of the South African political situation in which she claims that whites should play only a marginal role, in her early novels, including *July's People*, her main characters are white. In her fiction, Gordimer does not speak for black South Africans, but rather represents the predicament of whites, especially liberal whites, who benefit from a system they cannot morally support. While these characters are the central focus of her fiction, they are placed within a larger political context in which their choices have little effect, reflecting the marginal position Gordimer proposes for whites in *The Essential Gesture*.

July's People describes the near future, when a war has started in South Africa between the white government and the blacks. Having waited too long to leave the country, the Smales are trapped and flee from their house in the suburbs of Johannesburg in their *bakkie*, a small van, with their two children and their servant, July. The Smales are a nice, liberal couple; they have treated July well, by their standards. July takes them to his family's village in the bush. Here, the Smales try to fit themselves into village life, but ultimately they fail; only their children seem able to adapt. The novel focuses on Maureen Smales and her interactions with July, with her family, and with the village's people.

The narrative is given from a limited omniscient, third person perspective. Gordimer is hesitant in this novel to enter the minds of her black characters, and only does so on a few occasions. The narrator of *July's People* describes Maureen's vision of the village as follows: "Beyond the clearing—the settlement of huts, livestock kraals, and the stumped and burned-off patches which were the lands—the buttock-fold in the trees indicated the river and that was the end of measured distance" (*July's People* 26). Maureen is only able to "see" areas which are marked off by human boundaries, such as the cleared space of the village. The savannah beyond is unstable and constantly changing: "Like clouds, the savannah bush formed and re-formed under the changes of light, moved or gave the impression of being moved past by the travelling eye; silent and ashy green as mould spread and always spreading, rolling out under the sky before her" (26). This passage reflects Maureen's lack of perspective. Is the bush moving, or is it merely the movement of her vision? Even though she is standing still, the savannah seems to be "spreading, rolling out," a description which emphasizes instability. She then lists everything which can't be seen in the landscape: the trails, the villages of other people, the cattle, and the wild animals. The passage ends: "Space; so confining in its immensity her children did not know it was there" (26). This paradoxical "confining immensity" represents Maureen's inability to place herself in this new landscape. With a horizon this large and this alien, no place seems any different from any other; there is no escape.

Maureen's lack of perspective in spatial terms leads to a distortion of her sense of time: "Maureen was aware, among them in the hut, of not knowing where she was, in time, in the order of a day as she had always known it" (*July's People* 17). Her temporal dislocation intensifies her sense of being cut off from the familiar world.

As John Cooke has observed, Maureen's "very method of looking for a context by picturing a world she perceives as separate from herself . . . makes it impossible for her to make the transition to the veld" (Cooke 168). Maureen is used to being an observer rather than an actor. Gordimer gives a similar description of herself and her brother in "A South African Childhood: Allusions in a Landscape." During a trip to Kruger Park, they come upon an elephant and get out of their truck to photograph him: "I don't think he seemed real to us; we thought only of the camera, and saw the elephant as he would loom on the screen rather than as he was, a slack-skinned splendid hulk, standing there before us" ("Childhood" 125). Maureen, however, has no camera, and no audience "back there" to whom she could show her pictures. Her separation from the landscape serves only to isolate her.

Maureen tends to "keep to the paths," to restrict her horizon to the areas near the village: "Maureen could not walk out into the boundlessness" (*July's People* 27). She sees the bush as threatening, particularly at night. She sees "the forest smudge away in darkness that stepped closer in every interval of her attention" (46). The novel emphasizes her attempts to see, and to control by seeing. Her feeling that the darkness comes closer when she looks away from it is particularly unsettling to Maureen. She prefers to stay in areas with defined boundaries: the cleared lands, the yard between the houses, and within her house.

Maureen and Bamford Smales have trouble adapting to the land because they continue to use "back there" as a reference. Maureen's use of metaphors shows her reliance on household objects to provide a reference: "The gauze round of moon had become opaque and polished with the light of the vanished sun; it began gently to reflect, a mirror being adjusted" (*July's People* 150); "the firelight of their party was a pocket torch held under the blanket of the universe" (47). The objects from Johannesburg are manmade, small, and fragile: gauze, a mirror, a pocket torch. What they describe is immense: the moon, the night sky. The use of metaphor here shows Maureen's refusal to let go of the reference points of her former life, which are inadequate to describe this new landscape.

Bamford Smales has a similar difficulty in adjusting to this new life: "He struggled hopelessly for words that were not phrases from back there, words that would make the truth that must be forming here, out of the blacks, out of themselves. He sensed for a moment the great drama hidden in the monotonous days. . . . But the words would not come. They were blocked by the old vocabulary" (*July's People* 127). Their continued references to life back there, their use of "the old vocabulary," keep them from being able to see or to articulate "the truth which must be forming here."

Another factor which prevents Maureen from coming to terms with the landscape is her lack of work. Early in the novel she is described as moving between the houses of the village, "neither working as others did nor able to do nothing as others did" (*July's People* 28). At one point, she tries to go out gathering wild spinach with the women of the village. In this act she is trying to find a role for herself and hopes to become a part of the women's community. This would give her a relationship to the society and also to the land, for the women seem to her to be part of the landscape, like the birds: as they gather the wild greens, they are "keeping the pattern of a flock of egrets, that rises and settles now here, now there, where the pickings are best" (92). The narrator also pictures these women's lives as closer to the rhythms of the natural landscape. The only disturbance in July's wife's cycle of seasonal activities, for example, occurs when July comes home on his infrequent holidays: "Across the seasons was laid the diuturnal one of being without a man; it overlaid sowing and harvesting, rainy summers and dry winters, and at different times. . . . The sun rises, the moon sets; the money must come, the man must go" (83).

The black women's "natural" relationship to the land and their fatalistic attitude are over-emphasized here. As Paul Binding comments, Gordimer's black characters sometimes become "picturesque" (Binding 18) in their behavior and language. Yet in most cases, as in the description of the women gathering wild spinach, the description of the black women as integrated with the landscape is not a direct authorial comment on black women's relationship to the land. Rather, it is an indirect reflection of Maureen's thoughts about the women. Even as she attempts to join them, she feels herself to be an outsider: "At first the women in the fields ignored her. . . . One or two—the younger ones—perhaps remarked on her to each other as they would of someone come to remark upon them—a photographer, an overseer" (*July's People* 91). As she cannot speak their language, her attempt to become a part of the women's community fails. July reinforces this point by rebuking her for gathering greens, saying "The women have their work. They must do it. This is their place" (96-97). Maureen reflects on this speech, thinking: "He might mean 'place' in the sense of role, or might be implying she must remember she had no claim to the earth— 'place' as territory" (97). The ambiguity of the word "place" captures the connection between the social community and the landscape; without a place in society, Maureen has no place in the landscape.

At the end of the novel, Maureen hears a helicopter land somewhere in the bush. The helicopter could belong to either the white or black armies; Maureen is unable to see it. She seems to feel, however, that being rescued or being killed will be at least an escape from the village:

She runs: trusting herself with all the suppressed trust of a lifetime, alert, like a solitary animal at the season when animals neither seek a mate nor take care of young, existing only for their lone survival, the enemy of all that would make claims of responsibility. She can still hear the beat, beyond those trees and those, and she runs towards it. She runs. (*July's People* 160)

If we look at Maureen's actions as an answer to the question, "Where do whites fit in?" the answer is nowhere. Maureen runs into the bush, but only in hopes of running out of the landscape entirely. Despite her efforts, she has no place in the community, and no relationship to the land. Gordimer does offer some hope, however, in her depiction of the Smales' children. They have learned the language of the village, have made friends, and have found a place for themselves within the African society: "Gina was at home among the chickens, hearth ashes and communal mealie-meal pots of July's place" (*July's People* 121). The children, able to forget the landscape back there, can learn to adapt to the village.

July's People critiques white South African relationships to the land. As one anonymous reviewer comments, "There are white citizens of South Africa but no 'citizens' of the land itself any more. There are only claims on the landscape, made in words too loaded to be shared beyond the circle of one's own kind, one's own 'people'" (X 14). The Smales' claims to the landscape disintegrate with their house in the suburbs, while the relationship of July's "people" to the land can only be shared with their children, and not with them. Each group's claim excludes the other's, de-legitimizes it. Abdul JanMohammad analyzes this situation in *Manichean Aesthetics*:

By deliberately situating her fiction within the gap between apartheid theory and actual practice, between liberal pretense and actual callowness, and by repeatedly examining the conflict between the desire to leave and to stay, Gordimer's fiction simultaneously reveals the absence of and the desire for a viable, humane, and just interracial community which would free the individual from the debilitating contradictions of a manichean society. (JanMohammad 271)

While the novel is set in the future, the landscape reveals the contours of contemporary South Africa. The exposure of the limited horizon of "back there" serves as a warning to the whites of South Africa, while the immensity and formlessness of the bush in Maureen's eyes suggests the lack of an adequate vision of how whites will fit into South African society in the future. The outcome of the novel, Maureen's flight into the unknown, is an ominous prediction of the future of whites in South Africa.

J. M. COETZEE

J. M. Coetzee's work is very different from either Brink's or Gordimer's novels. Set in environments that could be, but aren't identified as, South Africa, his early novels are postmodern in tone and technique. Less realistic, less representative of a social world, they focus intensely on the perspective and psychological state of a single character. In this, they replicate the isolation and alienation of whites in South Africa. By not naming South Africa (except in *Age of Iron*), Coetzee implies that there is something that is not necessarily historically or geographically specific in the predicaments he explores. Whites in South Africa may be only the most visible example of the modern world's uneasy and compromising relationship to authority. "National security" is not used by South Africans alone to justify oppression.

Like *July's People*, J. M. Coetzee's *Waiting for the Barbarians* is set in a time and place outside of present-day South Africa. Set in the last days of the Empire, the novel describes the life of a magistrate in a border town along the frontier. Beyond this frontier lie the barbarians, who, the military claims, are massing for an attack. A military intelligence officer, Colonel Joll, comes to the town and tortures prisoners in order to extract the "truth." The magistrate, who tells the story, tries not to be present for these sessions, but finally cannot ignore them. He refuses to cooperate, and is himself taken prisoner and tortured. The novel centers on the magistrate's affair with a barbarian girl. She has been tortured by interrogators, and by washing her scarred body the magistrate attempts to make some reparation, to understand her suffering, and to understand the actions of her torturers.

The magistrate tells the story in the first person and in the present tense. This gives the novel a restricted horizon; unlike *The Grass Is Singing* or *July's People*, *Waiting for the Barbarians* allows the reader only the magistrate's perspective. He is a man whose dreams of a peaceful life have been thwarted by the chain of events:

I did not mean to get embroiled in this. I am a country magistrate, a responsible official in the service of the Empire, serving out my days on this lazy frontier, waiting to retire. I collect the tithes and taxes, administer the communal lands, see that the garrison is provided for. ... For the rest I watch the sun rise and set, eat and sleep and am content. ... I have not asked for more than a quiet life in quiet times. (*Waiting* 8)

He leads a cultured life, reading the classics, excavating ruins, collating maps of the region, hunting, enjoying fine food and wine. His life is partly responsive to the natural world: he has daily habits, and seasonal occupations. He comes to realize, however, that this civilized life is only possible because of the Empire: "I was the lie that Empire tells itself when times are easy, he the truth that Empire tells when harsh winds blow. Two sides of imperial rule, no more, no less" (135). Placed within the larger horizon of the Empire, the magistrate's seemingly harmless activities are revealed to be based on a system of oppression.

The attitude of the Empire and the military officers towards the land is one of domination and power. A young officer explains: "Even if it became necessary to supply the settlement by convoy, we would not go. Because these border settlements are the first line of defence of the Empire. The sooner the barbarians understand that the better" (*Waiting* 52). Seeing the borderland as the first line of defense, the Empire is unable to compromise, to seek a resolution other than the obliteration of the barbarians.

In an impassioned speech to this officer, the magistrate sympathizes with the barbarians' claims to the land:

We think of the country here as ours, part of our Empire —our outpost, our settlement, our market centre. But these people . . . still think of us as visitors, tran-
sients. There are old folk alive among them who remember their parents telling them
about this oasis as it once was: a well-shaded place by the side of the lake with plenty
of grazing even in winter. That is how they still talk about it, perhaps how they still
see it, as though not one spadeful of earth had been turned or one brick laid on top of
another. (*Waiting* 51)

In this image, the magistrate shows how the town, which from the Empire's
perspective is a permanent fortress, may be seen by the barbarians as merely
temporary. He imagines that their perspective is much larger, going beyond the
rise and fall of the Empire to the way the land was before the Empire came, and
how it will be after it falls. In the distant past, and in the distant future, the land
belongs to them. All they have to do is wait.

The magistrate's relationship to the land is complex. He is keenly aware of
the changing seasons, describing the coming of winters and springs with particular emphasis. He loves the land: "[I] stare out hungrily over the beloved landscape: the belt of green stretching along the river, blackened now in patches; the
lighter green of the marshes where the new reeds are shooting; the dazzling surface of the lake" (*Waiting* 97). In this short description, the references to color,
shape, and light reveals the magistrate's almost painterly appreciation of the
landscape. He also indicates the season in noticing the "new reeds." His perspective is practical, appreciative, yet accurate—he notices the blackened patches.

Beyond the immediate area around the town, however, the magistrate feels
that the land is threatening. As in Gordimer's works, Coetzee's novel shows
that the dominant race may feel that not only the oppressed people, but the land
itself, wishes to be rid of them: "The wind never lets up. It howls at us across
the ice, blowing from nowhere to nowhere. . . . The terrain is more desolate
than anything we have yet seen" (*Waiting* 60). Finally, the magistrate has to
conclude, despite his love for the land, that his life is inextricably associated
with the town: "There is nothing for me outside the walls but to starve" (101).

The town itself is seen as a series of enclosures: walls surrounding buildings
which in turn surround a courtyard. Within this town, there are yet other enclosures, such as the interrogation room:

I kneel down to examine the floor. It is clean, it is swept daily, it is like the floor of
any room. Above the fireplace on the wall and ceiling there is soot. There is also a
mark the size of my hand where soot has been rubbed into the wall. Otherwise the
walls are blank. What signs can I be looking for? (*Waiting* 35).

The magistrate's skills in accurate perception, which reveal clues in the landscape, fail in perceiving anything in the room which is able to indicate the horror of what happens there. The clues here are not in the "landscape" of the room,
but in the institutions of the Empire and the personalities of those who carry out
orders.

The magistrate is imprisoned by the military for treasonous consort with the enemy—his journey to return the barbarian girl to her people. The magistrate lies in his cell, hoping that this will somehow be the last time anyone is imprisoned here, yet he is listening to the sound of workers building a new, more secure prison next door:
"I pray for the day when these walls will be levelled and the unquiet echoes can finally take wing; though it is hard to ignore the sound of brick being laid on brick so nearby" (*Waiting* 80). The magistrate escapes from his prison cell for an evening, and finds a route out of the town: "The next door leads to my old apartment upstairs. It is locked. The third and last door stands open. . .   . I creep towards the dim blue square of the barred window, fearful of stumbling over the bodies whose breathing I hear all about me" (90). This description, with its locked rooms and barred windows, shows that the magistrate's cell is not the only enclosed space within the town. These bars and locks have been put in place by the inhabitants; they are creating their own cells. Coetzee illustrates this brilliantly in his descriptions of the inhabitants' reactions as fear of a barbarian invasion increases:

Before darkness falls the last goat must be brought in, the gates barred, a watch set in every lookout to call the hours. All night, it is said, the barbarians prowl about bent on murder and rapine. . . . The barbarians have dug a tunnel under the walls, people say; they come and go as they please, take what they like; no one is safe any longer. The farmers still till the fields, but they go out in bands, never singly. (*Waiting* 122).

The repetition throughout this passage of "it is said" and "people say" reveals the magistrate's skepticism about these claims; they are artificially created fears. Thus the town cuts itself off from its surroundings, creating a *laager* for a siege that may never come.

The magistrate's vision of the future is, like the barbarians', closely associated with the past. He has been excavating some ruins near the town, ruins which suggest to him that the present town is merely one repetition of an endless cycle: "Perhaps in bygone days criminals, slaves, soldiers trekked the twelve miles to the river, and cut down poplar trees . . . so that their masters, their prefects and magistrates and captains, could climb the roofs and towers morning and evening to scan the world from horizon to horizon for signs of the barbarians" (*Waiting* 15). The sense of time repeating itself is linked to the idea expressed earlier, that eventually the town will be recovered by the barbarians.

The magistrate tries to prepare a record of these events for future generations. His first attempt at describing the town is a failure: "We lived in the time of the seasons, of the harvests, of the migrations of the waterbirds. We lived with nothing between us and the stars. We would have made any concession, had we only known what, to go on living here. This was paradise on earth" (*Waiting* 154). This description is not of the real town, but rather of the ideal relationship to the land which the magistrate has wanted to establish, but which is falsified by his role in the Empire, and by his collusion with the oppressors. After composing these lines, the magistrate thinks, "When the barbarian is truly at the gate, perhaps then I will abandon the locutions of a civil servant with literary ambitions and begin to tell the truth" (154). This passage, in a self-reflexive move familiar in postmodernist texts, seems to suggest that the magistrate is undermining his own speech; if the novel is the unsatisfactory journal, the one which includes the "locutions of a civil servant," it is a lie. The piece he rejects, however, is clearly not a piece of this narrative that the reader holds in hand. Is it a lie, or does the novel represent the "true" journal, written later? By the end of the novel, the magistrate has not yet reached that truthful moment; he is "like a man who lost his way long ago but presses on along a road that may lead nowhere" (*Waiting* 156). Coetzee does not indicate whether the novel itself is the magistrate's representation of truth (and could this character, compromised and fearful, represent truth?) or the record of "a road that may lead nowhere." Unlike Brink in *A Dry White Season*, Coetzee problematizes the relationship of his text to reality, removing it from time and geographical space, and foregrounding the unreliability of his narrator.

Waiting for the Barbarians sets up dichotomies between the walled town and the limitless desert, between the Empire's and the barbarians' vision of the land. These dichotomies are all expressed by a single narrator, however, and so the problems Gordimer had with describing the black African's relation to the landscape are avoided. Coetzee is reporting what the magistrate thought that the barbarians felt about the land. There is an additional distance from the real historical situation in South Africa, of course, through his use of an imaginary Empire and barbarians, rather than the South African Government and the Africans. While this solves some problems, it raises others. As Irving Howe notes: "To create a 'universalized' Empire is to court the risk . . . that a narrative with strong political and social references will be 'elevated' into sterile ruminations about the human condition" (Howe 36). By avoiding direct description of the South African situation, Coetzee's critique may appear more diffuse, less pointed at the particular issues of race and oppression in South Africa. Yet it is still a powerful critique of oppression, torture, and imperialism, and it shows how the ruling faction is able to gain the acquiescence of the populace. One could extend the implications of the magistrate's position to anyone who tries to ignore the actions of the South African Government.

CONCLUSION

While all three novelists express an attachment to the land, their characters often see it as threatening, savage, or inhuman. When they are out on the veld, they feel exposed, vulnerable, and afraid; when they are inside, they become aware of their own enclosure, not only by walls but by social restrictions and laws, to the point of claustrophobia. The choices presented to them are extreme: for Ben Du Toit and the magistrate, acquiescence or rebellion; for Maureen, alienation or flight. None of the novels describes a middle ground, a way of living with the contemporary contradictions of South Africa. None offers a specific plan of action, or vision of future harmony; whereas Ngugi's Wariinga strides into the future, Maureen Smales flees into the bush. The image we are left with is of

Select Bibliography

PRIMARY TEXTS

Achebe, Chinua. *Things Fall Apart*. London: Heinemann, 1986.

Alkali, Zaynab. *The Stillborn*. London: Longman, 1988.

Armah, Ayi Kwei. *The Beautyful Ones Are Not Yet Born*. Toronto: Collier (Macmillan), 1969.

Bâ, Mariama. *So Long a Letter*. Trans. by Modupé Bodé-Thomas. London: Heinemann, 1981.

Brink, André. *A Dry White Season*. New York: Penguin, 1984.

Clark-Bekederemo, J. P. "Ibadan." In *Collected Plays and Poems 1958-1988*. p. 318. Washington DC: Howard University Press, 1991.

Coetzee, J. M. *Age of Iron*. New York: Random House, 1990.

_____. *Waiting for the Barbarians*. New York: Penguin, 1982.

Conrad, Joseph. *Heart of Darkness: A Case Study in Contemporary Criticism*. Ed. by Ross C. Murfin. New York: St. Martin's, 1989.

Dinesen, Isak. *Out of Africa*. New York: Century Publishers, 1985.

Emecheta, Buchi. *The Joys of Motherhood*. New York: George Braziller, 1979.

Gordimer, Nadine. *July's People*. New York: Penguin, 1982.

Head, Bessie. *A Gesture of Belonging: Letters from Bessie Head, 1965-1979*. Ed. by Randolph Vigne. London: Heinemann, 1991.

_____. *Maru*. London: Heinemann, 1972.

_____. *A Question of Power*. London: Heinemann, 1974.

_____. *A Woman Alone: Autobiographical Writings*. Ed. by Craig MacKenzie. London: Heinemann, 1990.

Kane, Cheikh Hamidou. *Ambiguous Adventure*. Trans. by Katherine Woods. London: Heinemann, 1972.

La Guma, Alex. *A Walk in the Night and Other Stories*. Evanston: Northwestern University Press, 1968.

Laye, Camara. *The African Child*. Trans. by James Kirkup. London: Collins, 1959.

Lessing, Doris. *The Grass Is Singing*. New York: Plume, 1976.

Matshoba, Mtutuzeli. *Call Me Not a Man: the Stories of Mtutuzeli Matshoba*. Johannesburg: Ravan Press, 1979.

Ngugi wa Thiong'o. *Devil on the Cross*. London: Heinemann, 1978.
_____. *Matigari*. Trans. by Wangui wa Goro. Oxford: Heinemann, 1989.
_____. *Petals of Blood*. New York: E.P. Dutton, 1982.
_____. *The River Between*. London: Heinemann, 1965.
Okri, Ben. *The Landscapes Within*. Harlow: Longman, 1984.
Ramgobin, Mewa. *Waiting to Live*. Cape Town: David Philip, 1986.
Rive, Richard. *Buckingham Palace: District Six*. Cape Town: David Philip, 1986.
Serote, Mongane. *To Every Birth Its Blood*. London: Heinemann, 1983.
Soyinka, Wole. *Aké: The Years of Childhood*. New York: Vintage (Random House), 1989.
Tlali, Miriam. *Amandla*. Johannesburg: Ravan Press, 1980.
_____. *Mihloti*. Johannesburg: Skotaville Publishers, 1984.
_____. *Muriel at Metropolitan*. Harlow: Longman, 1987.
Tutuola, Amos. *The Palm-Wine Drinkard and his Dead Palm-Wine Tapster in the Dead's Town*. New York: Grove Press, 1984.

SECONDARY TEXTS

Abrahams, Cecil, ed. *The Tragic Life: Bessie Head and Literature in Southern Africa*. Trenton: Africa World Press, 1990.
Abrahams, Peter. "A Literary Pioneer." Review of *People of the City* by Cyprian Ekwensi. *West Africa* (16 Oct. 1954): 975.
Adler, Michelle, Susan Gardner, Tobeka Mda and Patricia Sandler. Interview with Bessie Head in *Between the Lines: Interviews with Bessie Head, Sheila Roberts, Ellen Kuzwayo, Miriam Tlali*. Ed. by Craig MacKenzie and Cherry Clayton, pp. 5-30. Grahamstown, South Africa: National English Literary Museum, 1989.
Aidoo, Ama Ata. Interview in *In Their Own Voices*. Adeola James, 9-27, 1990.
Anderson, Benedict. *Imagined Communities: Reflections on the Origin and Spread of Nationalism.*, rev. ed. London: Verso, 1991.
Asein, S. O. and A. O. Ashaolu, eds. *Studies in the African Novel*. Ibadan: Ibadan University Press, 1986.
Beetham, David. "The Future of the Nation State." In *The Idea of the Modern State*. Ed. by Gregor McLennan, David Held and Stuart Hall, pp. 208-222. Buckingham: Open University Press, 1984.
Benstock, Shari. "Expatriate Modernism: Writings on the Cultural Rim" in *Women's Writing in Exile*. Ed. by Mary Lynn Broe and Angela Ingram, pp. 19-40, 1989.
Bhabha, Homi K., ed. *Nation and Narration*. London: Routledge, 1990.
Binding, Paul. "Unrealised." Review of *July's People* by Nadine Gordimer. *New Statesman* 102 (11 Sept. 1981): 18-19.
Bishop, Rand. *African Literature, African Critics: The Forming of Critical Standards 1947-1966*.Westport, CT: Greenwood Press, 1988.
Boehmer, Elleke. "Stories of Women and Mothers: Gender and Nationalism in the Early Fiction of Flora Nwapa." in *Motherlands* Ed. by Susheila Nasta, pp. 3-23, 1992.
Brink, André. *Writing in a State of Siege: Essays on Politics and Literature*. New York: Summit Books (Simon & Schuster), 1983.
Broe, Mary Lynn and Angela Ingram, eds. *Women's Writing in Exile*. Chapel Hill: University of North Carolina Press, 1989.
Butler, Judith. *Bodies That Matter: On the Discursive Limits of "Sex."* New York: Routledge, 1993.
Carpenter, William. "The Scene of Representation in Alex La Guma's Later Novels." *English in Africa* 18, no. 2 (October 1991): 1-18.
Chima, Alex. "Culture and Politics in Africa." *Africa and the World* 2, no. 22 (1966): 29-31. Quoted in Bishop p. 123.

Chinweizu, Onwuchekwa Jemie and Ihechukwu Madubuike. *Toward the Decolonization of African Literature: African Fiction and Poetry and Their Critics*. London: KPI, 1985.

Clark, J. P. "Aspects of Nigerian Drama." *Nigeria Magazine* 89 (1966): 118-126.

Coetzee, J.M. "Man's Fate in the Novels of Alex La Guma." *Studies in Black Literature* 5, no. 1 (1974): 16-23.

_____. *White Writing: On the Culture of Letters in South Africa*. New Haven: Yale University Press, 1988.

Cooke, John. *The Novels of Nadine Gordimer: Private Lives/Public Landscapes*. Baton Rouge: Louisiana State University Press, 1985.

Courtney-Clarke, Margaret. *African Canvas: The Art of West African Women*. New York: Rizzoli, 1991.

Daymond, M. J. "The Lost Community." Review of *Buckingham Palace: District Six* by Richard Rive. *Reality: A Journal of Liberal and Radical Opinion* 19, no. 2 (March 1987): 18-19.

Driver, Dorothy. "Ma-Ngoana O Tsoare Thipa ka Bohaleng—The Child's Mother Grabs the Sharp End of the Knife: Women as Mothers, Women as Writers." In *Rendering Things Visible: Essays on South African Literary Culture*. Ed. by Martin Trump pp. 225-255 . Athens, OH: Ohio University Press, 1990.

DuPlessis, Rachel Blau. "For the Etruscans." In *The New Feminist Criticism: Essays on Women, Literature and Theory*. Ed. by Elaine Showalter, pp. 271-291. New York: Pantheon Books, 1985.

Eagleton, Terry, Fredric Jameson and Edward W. Said. *Nationalism, Colonialism and Literature*. Minneapolis: University of Minnesota Press, 1990.

Fido, Elaine Savory. "Mother/lands: Self and Separation in the Work of Buchi Emecheta, Bessie Head and Jean Rhys." in *Motherlands*. Ed. by Susheila Nasta, pp. 330-349, 1992.

Friedman, Susan Stanford. "Exile in the American Grain." In *Women's Writing in Exile*. Ed. by Mary Lynn Broe and Angela Ingram, pp. 87-112, 1989.

Gates, Henry Louis. *The Signifying Monkey: A Theory of African-American Literary Criticism*. New York: Oxford, 1988.

Gordimer, Nadine. *The Essential Gesture: Writing, Politics and Places*. New York: Alfred A. Knopf, 1988.

_____. "A South African Childhood: Allusions in a Landscape." *The New Yorker* 30 (16 Oct. 1954): 111-129.

_____. "Where Do Whites Fit In?" In *The Essential Gesture*, pp. 31-37, 1988.

Green, Robert. "Chopin in the Ghetto: The Short Stories of Alex La Guma." *World Literature Written in English* 20 (1981): 5-16.

Gurr, Andrew. *Writers in Exile: The Identity of Home in Modern Literature*. Atlantic Highlands, NJ: Humanities Press, 1981.

Haque, Shaheen. "The Politics of Space: The Experience of a Black Woman Architect." In *Charting the Journey: Writings by Black and Third World Women*. Ed. by Shabnam Grewal, Jackie Kay, Liliane Landor, Gail Lewis and Pratibha Parmar, pp. 34-39. London: Sheba Feminist Publishers, 1988.

Harrow, Kenneth. "Camara Laye, Cheikh Hamidou Kane, and Tayeb Salib: Three Sufi Authors." *In Faces of Islam in African Literature*. Ed. by Kenneth Harrow, pp. 261-297. Portsmouth, NH: Heinemann, 1991.

Hay, Margaret Jean and Sharon Stichter, eds. *African Women South of the Sahara*. London: Longman, 1984.

Hegel, Georg Wilhelm Friedrich. *The Philosophy of History*. Trans. by J. Sibree. New York: Dover Publications, 1956.

Herbst, Jeffrey. "Migration, the Politics of Protest, and State Consolidation in Africa." *African Affairs: The Journal of the Royal African Society* 89, no. 355 (April 1990): 183-204.

Hobsbawm, E. J. *Nations and Nationalism Since 1780: Programme, Myth, Reality.* Cambridge: Cambridge University Press, 1990.

Howe, Irving. "A Stark Political Fable of South Africa." Review of *Waiting for the Barbarians* by J.M. Coetzee. *The New York Times Book Review* (18 Apr. 1982): 1, 36.

Huxley, Elspeth. *The Flame Trees of Thika: Memories of An African Childhood.* New York: William Morrow, 1959.

_____. *White Man's Country: Lord Delamere and the Making of Kenya,* vol 1. London: Chatto and Windus, 1953.

Ikiddeh, Ime. "James Ngugi as novelist." *African Literature Today* 2 (1969): 3-10.

Irele, Abiola. *The African Experience in Literature and Ideology.* Bloomington: Indiana University Press, 1981; reprint 1990.

James, Adeola. *In Their Own Voices: African Women Writers Talk.* London: James Currey, 1990.

JanMohamed, Abdul R. *Manichean Aesthetics: The Politics of Literature in Colonial Africa.* Amherst: University of Massachusetts Press, 1983.

Johnson, Lemuel. Conversation about Buchi Emecheta, Brock University, Ontario, Canada, May 2, 1992.

_____. "Crescent and Consciousness: Islamic Orthodoxies and the West African Novel." In *Faces of Islam in African Literature.* Ed. by Kenneth Harrow, pp. 239-260. Portsmouth, NH: Heinemann, 1991.

July, Robert W. *A History of the African People,* 3rd. ed.. New York: Charles Scribner's Sons, 1980.

Kenyatta, Jomo. *Facing Mount Kenya: The Tribal Life of the Gikuyu.* London: Heinemann, 1961.

Kibera, Valerie. "Adopted Motherlands: The Novels of Marjorie Macgoye and Bessie Head." In *Motherlands.* Ed. by Susheila Nasta, pp. 310-329, 1992.

Kincaid, Jamaica. "On Seeing England For the First Time." *Transition: An International Review* 51: 32-40.

Larson, Charles R. *The Emergence of African Fiction.* rev. ed. Bloomington: Indiana University Press, 1972.

Lazarus, Neil. "Disavowing Decolonization: Fanon, Nationalism, and the Problematic of Representation in Current Theories of Colonial Discourse." *Research in African Literatures* 24, no.4 (Winter 1993): 69-98.

Lessing, Doris. "Desert Child." Review of *The Lost World of the Kalahari* by Laurens Van Der Post. *The New Statesman* 56 (15 Nov. 1958): 700.

Lockett, Cecily. Interview with Miriam Tlali in *Between the Lines: Interviews with Bessie Head, Sheila Roberts, Ellen Kuzwayo, Miriam Tlali.* Ed. by Craig MacKenzie and Cherry Clayton, pp. 69-85. Grahamstown, South Africa: National English Literary Museum, 1989.

Miller, Christopher. *Blank Darkness: Africanist Discourse in French.* Chicago: University of Chicago Press, 1985.

Moore, Gerald. "The Negro Poet and his Landscape." In *Introduction to African Literature.* Ed. by Ulli Beier, pp. 151-164. London: Longmans, Green & Co., 1967.

_____. *Seven African Writers.* London: Oxford University Press, 1962.

Mortimer, Mildred. *Journeys Through The French African Novel.* Portsmouth: Heinemann, 1990.

Mphahlele, Ezekiel. ". . . Away Into Ancestral Fields?" *Fighting Talk* 14 no. 1 (1960): 11-12. Quoted in Bishop 104.

_____. "Critic's Time for the Novel." *Conference of African Writers of English Expression.* Paris: Congress for Cultural Freedom, 1962. Quoted in Bishop 120.

_____. "Entretien avec Ezekiel Mphahlele." *Afrique* 17 (1962): 52-59. Quoted and translated by Bishop 37.

_____. "The Importance of Being Black." *New Leader* 43, no.41 (24 Oct 1960): 10-11. Quoted in Bishop 157-158.

Mudimbe, V. Y. *The Invention of Africa: Gnosis, Philosophy, and the Order of Knowledge.* Bloomington: Indiana University Press, 1988.

Nasta, Susheila, ed. *Motherlands: Black Women's Writing from Africa, the Caribbean and South Asia.* New Brunswick, NJ: Rutgers University Press, 1992.

Ngugi wa Thiong'o. *Decolonizing the Mind: The Politics of Language in African Literature.* London: James Currey, 1986.

_____. *Homecoming: Essays on African and Caribbean Literature, Culture and Politics.* New York: Heinemann, 1972.

_____. "Ngugi wa Thiong'o still bitter over his detention" *The Weekly Review.* No. 203 (5 Jan. 1979): 30-32.

_____. "On Writing in Gikuyu." *Research in African Literatures* 16, no. 2 (1985): 151-156.

Nnaemeka, Obioma. "From Orality to Writing: African Women Writers and the (Re)Inscription of Womanhood." *Research in African Literatures* 25, no.4 (1994): 137-157.

Nnolim, Charles E. "Background Setting: Key to the Structure of Ngugi's *The River Between*" *Obsidian* 2, No. 2 (1976): 20-29. Reprinted in *Critical Perspectives on Ngugi wa Thiong'o.* Ed. by G. D. Killam, pp. 136-145. Washington: Three Continents Press, 1984.

Obbo, Christine. *African Women: Their Struggle for Economic Independence.* London: Zed Press, 1980.

Obumselu, Ben. Review of *Things Fall Apart* by Chinua Achebe. *Ibadan* 5 (1959): 37-38.

Ojo-Ade, Femi. "Still A Victim? Mariama Bâ's *Une si Longue Lettre*" *African Literature Today* 12 (1982): 71-87.

Okasha, Sarwat (also known as Tharwat Ukashah). *The Muslim Painter and the Divine: The Persian Impact on Islamic Religious Painting.* London: Park Lane Press, 1981.

Okpewho, Isidore. *African Oral Literature: Backgrounds, Character, and Continuity.* Bloomington: Indiana University Press, 1992.

Rabkin, David. "La Guma and Reality in South Africa." *Journal of Commonwealth Literature* 8 (June 1973): 54-62.

Robson, Clifford B. *Ngugi Wa Thiong'o.* New York: St. Martin's Press, 1979.

Rodney, Walter. *How Europe Underdeveloped Africa.* London: Bogle-L'Ouverhure, 1972.

Roscoe, Adrian. *Mother Is Gold: A Study in West African Literature.* Cambridge: Cambridge University Press, 1971.

_____. *Uhuru's Fire: African Literature East to South.* Cambridge: Cambridge University Press, 1977.

Rushdie, Salman. "Imaginary Homelands." In *Imaginary Homelands: Essays and Criticism 1981-1991*, pp. 9-21. London: Granta-Penguin, 1991.

Said, Edward W. *Culture and Imperialism.* New York: Vintage Books, 1994.

_____. "Yeats and Decolonization." In *Nationalism Colonialism and Literature* by Terry Eagleton, Fredric Jameson and Edward Said, pp. 69-95. Minneapolis: University of Minnesota Press, 1990.

Senghor, Leopold. "L'Afrique noire." In *Les Plus Beaux Ecrits de L'Union française et du Maghreb.* Presented by Mohamed El Kholti, Leopold Sedar Senghor, Pierre Do Dinh, A. Rakoto Ratsimamanga, and E. Ralajmihiatra. Paris: La Colombe, 1947, pp. 163-262. Quoted and translated by Bishop 95.

Sole, Kelwyn. "'This Time Set Again:' The Temporal and Political Conceptions of Serote's *To Every Birth Its Blood.*" *English in Africa* 18, no. 1 (May 1991): 51-80.

Soyinka, Wole. *Myth, Literature and the African World.* Cambridge: Canto-Cambridge University Press, 1990.

Spivak, Gayatri Chakravorty. *In Other Worlds: Essays in Cultural Politics.* New York and London: Methuen, 1987.

Taiwo, Oladele. *Female Novelists of Modern Africa.* New York: St Martin's Press, 1984.

Thelwell, Michael. "Introduction." In *The Palm-Wine Drinkard* by Amos Tutuola. New York: Grove Press, 1984.

Thomas, Dylan. "Blithe Spirits." Review of *The Palm-Wine Drinkard* by Amos Tutuola. *Observer* (6 July 1952): 7. Quoted in Bishop 36.

Tlali, Miriam. Interview in *Between the Lines: Interviews with Bessie Head, Sheila Roberts, Ellen Kuzwayo, Miriam Tlali.* Ed. by Craig MacKenzie and Cherry Clayton, pp.71-85. Grahamstown, South Africa: National English Literary Museum, 1989.

Trump, Martin. "Serote's *To Every Birth Its Blood* and Debates within Southern Africa's Literature of Liberation." *Staffrider* 9, no. 2 (1990): 37-49.

Wanjala, Chris. *The Season of Harvest: Some Notes on East African Literature.* Nairobi: Kenya Literature Bureau, 1978.

Wicomb, Zoë. "To Hear the Variety of Discourses." *Current Writing: Text and Reception in Southern Africa* 2 (October 1990): 35-44.

Woolf, Virginia. *Three Guineas.* New York and London: Harcourt Brace Jovanovich, 1966.

"X" [pseud.]. "Fall of a House." Review of *July's People* by Nadine Gordimer. *New York Review of Books* 28 (13 Aug. 1981): 14-18.

Young, Iris Marion. "Throwing Like a Girl: A Phenomenology of Feminine Body Comportment, Motility, and Spatiality." In *The Thinking Muse: Feminism and Modern French Philosophy.* Ed. by Jeffner Allen and Iris Marion Young, pp. 51-70. Bloomington: Indiana University Press, 1989.

Index

Abrahams, Cecil, 93
Abrahams, Peter, 56
Achebe, Chinua, 5, 7, 23, 24, 55, 58-61, 63, 67-69; *Things Fall Apart*, 7, 55, 58-61, 63, 67-69
Aidoo, Ama Ata, 38, 53
Alkali, Zaynab, 49-53
Anderson, Benedict, 6, 8
Architecture, rural, 43, 50-51; urban, 39, 41, 43
Armah, Ayi Kwei, 58, 68, 69; *The Beautyful Ones Are Not Yet Born*, 68
Asein, S. O, 73

Bâ, Mariama, 44-48, 53
Bhabha, Homi K., 7, 10-11, 15 n.3, n.5
Boehmer, Elleke, 9, 37, 53, 85
Brink, André, 12, 95, 101, 102-105, 113; *A Dry White Season*, 101, 102-105, 113; *Writing in a State of Siege*, 104-105
Butler, Judith, 14

Chinweizu, Onwuchekwa Jemie, 2, 3, 55

Clark, J. P., 3, 14-15 n.2, 33 n.2, 59
Coetzee, J.M., 12, 76-77, 78, 101, 105, 109-113; *Age of Iron*, 109; *Waiting for the Barbarians*, 101, 105, 109-113; *White Writing*, 12
Colonialism, 4, 5, 6-9, 10-11, 17-19, 21, 23-24, 26-27, 31-33, 37, 39, 42-43, 55, 58, 62, 67, 68, 69, 82
Conrad, Joseph, 2, 3, 7

Dinesen, Isak, 2, 60
Driver, Dorothy, 88
DuPlessis, Rachel Blau, 9, 10, 12

Ekwensi, Cyprian, 37, 68
Emecheta, Buchi, 11, 38-44, 53, 83
Exile, 10-12, 32-33, 44, 82-83, 85-86, 92, 97-99, 101

Fido, Elaine Savory, 38, 97
Friedman, Susan Stanford, 85

Gates, Henry Louis, 14 n.1
Gordimer, Nadine, 11, 101, 102, 105-109, 111, 113; *July's People*, 101, 105-109;

"Where Do Whites Fit In?" 102, 109
Gurr, Andrew, 19, 25

Head, Bessie, 10, 11-12, 38, 73, 85-86, 92-99
Hegel, Georg Wilhelm Friedrich, 24
Homelands, 71, 73-75, 89, 101
Horizon, 4-5, 8-13, 31, 41, 42, 44, 49, 53, 54, 62, 64, 67, 69, 72, 77-78, 82-84, 86, 95, 106-107, 109, 110, 112
Huxley, Elspeth, 18

Imperialism, 5-8, 10, 12, 27, 53, 78, 110, 113
Irele, Abiola, 70 n.1

JanMohamed, Abdul R., 109
Johnson, Lemuel, 42, 65

Kane, Cheikh Hamidou, 13, 55, 65-67, 69
Kenyatta, Jomo, 18, 21

La Guma, Alex, 11, 75-78, 83
Larson, Charles, 1-2
Laye, Camara, 35
Lessing, Doris, 11, 101

Matshoba, Mtutuzeli, 74-75
Men and exile, 11, 82-83; and landscape description, 55-69, 71-84; and nationalism, 9, 69, 92; and religion, 55-69
Miller, Christopher, 2, 10
Moore, Gerald, 23, 58
Mortimer, Mildred, 48
Mphahlele, Ezekiel, 56, 72
Mudimbe, V. Y., 36

Nationalism, 5, 6-10, 11, 13, 19, 22-24, 27, 37-38, 40, 42, 44, 53, 69, 85, 92, 93, 102, 110
Ngugi wa Thiong'o, 2, 4, 5, 8, 11-12, 17-33, 37, 55, 113; Decolonizing the Mind, 24; Devil on the Cross, 28-31;

Homecoming, 17, 19, 22, 24, 27; Matigari, 31-33; Petals of Blood, 19, 24-30; The River Between, 2, 19-25, 27, 33, 37
Nnaemeka, Obioma, 36, 38

Okpewho, Isidore, 28, 32
Okri, Ben, 58, 68-69

Precolonial Africa, 4-8, 13, 36
Postcolonial landscapes, 3-5, 39, 68, 98

Ramgobin, Mewa, 74
Religion and landscape, 4, 6, 7, 12-13, 20-22, 25, 28, 30, 36, 37, 44-45, 47, 49-51, 55-69
Rive, Richard, 72, 78-79, 83
Rodney, Walter, 6
Roscoe, Adrian, 1-2, 15 n.2, 20, 33-34 n.2, 77

Said, Edward W., 6-8, 15 n.4
Senghor, Leopold, 60
Serote, Mongane, 80-83
Sole, Kelwyn, 82-83
South Africa, 6, 8, 10-12, 71-113
Soyinka, Wole, 4, 13, 56, 58, 62-65, 67, 68-69; Aké: The Years of Childhood, 55-56, 62-65; Myth, Literature and the African World, 13
Spivak, Gayatri Chakravorty, 9-10

Tlali, Miriam, 3, 10, 73, 83, 85-92, 98-99
Townships, 12, 73-84, 101, 103
Tutuola, Amos, 55, 56-58, 61, 69, 69-70 n.1
Trump, Martin, 82

Urban landscapes, 3, 38-41, 43, 68-69, 73-84

Wanjala, Chris, 23
Wicomb, Zoë, 95-96
White writers and landscape, 6, 12, 111-113

Women, 4, 9-13, 30, 35-53, 69;
        and exile, 11-12, 44, 85-86,
        92, 97-99; and landscape
        description, 35-53, 83, 85-99,
        105-109; and nationalism, 9-
        10, 37-38, 40, 42, 44, 53,
        85, 92, 93; and religion, 13,
        36, 37, 44-45, 47-50, 51
Woolf, Virginia, 9, 85

Young, Iris Marion, 47-48